Nature Library

WILD FLOWERS

Nature Library

WILD FLOWERS

Bob Press
Marian Short

Exeter Books

NEW YORK

Frontispiece: **Opium poppy.**

Artists

June Baker; Henry Barnett; Roger Gorringe; Leslie Greenwood; Michael Hodson Designs; Mei-Lan Lim; Kenneth Oliver.

Photographic acknowledgements

A-Z COLLECTION, DORKING 10 bottom left, 11 top left, 24 top right, 25 bottom, 32 bottom right, 63 bottom, François Merlet 36, 65 bottom; HEATHER ANGEL BIOFOTOS, FARNHAM 11 bottom right, 14 top right, 19 top, 21 left top and bottom, 27 bottom, 41 left middle and bottom, 48 bottom, 62 middle, 72 top right, 74-5; BOTANICAL ENTERPRISES (PUBLICATIONS) LIMITED, BISHOP AUCKLAND 33 right top and bottom, 65 top left; FRED BREUMMER 17 bottom right; J. K. BURRAS 52; J. ALLAN CASH LIMITED, LONDON 46 right; BRUCE COLEMAN LIMITED, UXBRIDGE Bob and Clara Calhoun 24 bottom left, Robert P. Carr 14 top left, Eric Crichton 31, 32 bottom left, 51 top left, Gerald Cubitt 23 bottom, Nicholas de Vore 72 top left, M. P. L. Fogden 54 top right, Jennifer Fry 62 top, Udo Hirsch 32 top, Lee Lyon 61 third from top, Rocco Longo 34 bottom left, Norman Myers 54 bottom, Charlie Ott 12 top right, Prato 28 top, 65 top right, Hans Reinhard 18 bottom right, Lynn M. Stone 29, 30 top left and right, John Topham 10 right, G. D. Plage 45 bottom, Peter Ward 12 top left; W. F. DAVIDSON 26 top; ADRIAN DAVIES 6-7; MICHAEL DENT 39, 47 top right; FAO PHOTO, ROME 46 bottom right; KAREL FEUERSTEIN 56 top; JOHN B. FREE 13 top; CHRIS GREY WILSON 24 top left; G. HALL 55 bottom right; F. NIGEL HEPPER 16 top left; ROYSTON E. HEATH 18 left top and bottom, 19 bottom left and right; CHRIS HUMPHRIES 51 bottom, 70 bottom, 73 top left and bottom left and right; ALAN HUTCHISON LIBRARY 24 bottom right, 58 bottom, 61 middle right, Dr Nigel Smith 30 bottom; THOR LARSEN 16 bottom; AUDLEY MONEY-KYRLE 12 bottom; IAN MUGGERIDGE 47 top left; THE NATURAL HISTORY PHOTOGRAPHIC AGENCY—Brian Hawkes 2, M. Morcombe 51 middle, Ken Preston-Mafham 40, 61 bottom; J. REDITT 61 second from top; G. R. ROBERTS 33 top left; BRYAN SAGE 16-17 top; H. SMITH 71; BERNARD STONEHOUSE 72 bottom left; DAVID SUTTON 49 right top and bottom, 53 bottom, 68, 69 top, 73 bottom left and right; JØRN THOMASSEN 17 bottom left; JUDY TODD 9 middle left and right, 13 middle left, 14 bottom, 15 bottom left, 15 top right, 21 top right, 22 top left, 23 top right, 34 top left, 37, 43 top, 47 bottom left, 49 left, 59 bottom right, 62 bottom, 63 top; BRIAN TRODD 54 left top and middle; NEWNES BOOKS, FELTHAM—Adrian Davies 38 top, Peter Loughran 25 top right, 27 top left, 28 bottom, 38 bottom left, 41 bottom right, 42 top left, 44 top left and right top and bottom, 45 top, 60, 64 top and bottom, 66 left and right, 76-7.

Contents

Introduction

Plants are familiar things because they grow all around us. But plants do much more than just provide scenery – they are of vital importance to life on earth – so it is essential that we know and understand them.

Green plants are the only organisms capable of photosynthesis and are the first link in complex food-chains which support animals, including man. Of equal importance is one of the by-products of photosynthesis, oxygen, which is released into the air. We eat and breathe by courtesy of green plants!

In addition to food and oxygen, plants provide animals with homes, giving shelter and protection. Plants also protect the land itself, for without a covering of vegetation, soil and even rocks are soon eroded away.

There are several different groups of plants, for example algae, mosses and ferns, but only the angiosperms – the plants we think of as flowers – actually produce these structures. Angiosperms are the most complex and widespread of all the plant groups and have a range of adaptions which allows them to live in every part of the world.

As well as their economic importance to us, flowering plants are creations of matchless beauty and the world would be a poorer place without them. Their variety and sheer ability to survive is both intriguing and delightful. Concern for plants is, somewhat belatedly, growing and if we can learn to appreciate them their survival will be more assured.

In the following pages we have tried to show something of the variety of flowering plants and the habitats in which they can be found.

JRP
MJS

Dense cushions of thrift (*Armeria maritima*) on a coastal cliff.

Plant Structure

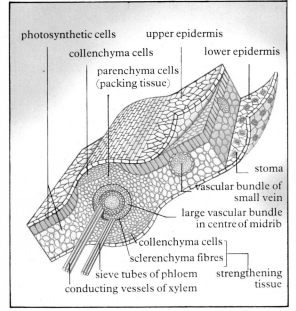

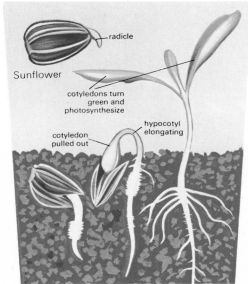

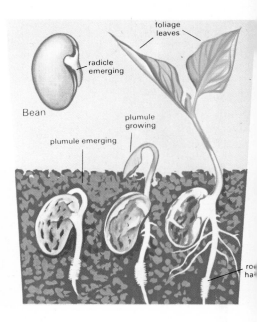

Above left **The complex structure of a leaf is shown in this three-dimensional diagram.**

Above **Sequences showing stages in different types of germination: hypocotyl– in which the cocotyledons emerge above the ground and act as first leaves; hypogeal in which they remain below the soil and the plumule bearing true leaves emerges instead.**

Far left **The colourful 'petals' of Bougainvillea are modified leaves.**

Left, above **The 'leaves' of butcher's broom are flattened stems.**

Left, below **The 'root' of Solomon's seal is an underground stem with real roots beneath.**

All flowering plants have the same basic parts — roots, stems, leaves and flowers — though any of these may be so highly modified that they are difficult to recognise for what they are.

Leaves. These are the factories of the plant. Their green colour is due to the pigment chlorophyll contained in chloroplasts which trap sunlight for use in photosynthesis. This is the process in which carbon dioxide from the air and water from the soil are combined using energy from the sun to make sugars. One of the by-proucts is oxygen which is released back into the air.

Leaves tend to be thin and flat. This shape allows the interception of maximum amounts of sunlight, and air can diffuse quickly to all parts of the leaf.

Water and nutrients are brought to the leaves by tissue called xylem while the sugars and other products are distributed from the leaves via phloem tissue. Together xylem and phloem form the conducting or vascular system of the plants, seen in the leaves as veins.

To prevent undue water loss, which causes wilting, the outside of the leaf is covered by a waterproof, waxy cuticle. As well as keeping water in, the cuticle keeps gases out; so there are special pores called stomata which allow air access to and from the centre of the leaf. The plant can control this access by using guard cells to open or close the stomata.

Stems. Stems have several functions. They support the leaves and flowers, holding them up into the sunlight. They also contain vascular tissue connecting the leaves and roots, allowing the passage of water and the products of photosynthesis between the two. Sometimes the vascular tissue becomes woody as in trees and shrubs, adding greatly to the strength of the stem.

Roots. The roots form a branching system which spreads through the soil, anchoring the plant firmly in place. Fine root-hairs absorb water and other nutrients from the soil to be sent via the stem to the leaves. Roots may also act as storehouses for the food produced by the leaves, to be held against times of need. Tap-roots and root-tubers are examples.

Germination. Seeds are protected by a tough coat. During germination the seed swells with water to split the coat and begin growth. The first root, or radicle, grows from the seed down into the soil. Next the seed-leaves or cotyledons may emerge and be lifted above the soil. Alternatively they may remain within the seed coat and the plumule — a shoot bearing true leaves — grows up instead.

Flowering plants are divided into two groups, depending on whether they have one or two cotyledons. The former are called monocots and include such plants as grasses, lilies and orchids. The latter are the dicots. The easiest way to tell them apart (other than looking at the seedlings) is to look at the leaf veins. In monocots they run parallel to each other. In dicots they form a network.

Lifespan. Plants can live for varying lengths of time—some trees are hundreds of years old — but most do not live for anything like as long. They can be divided into three types.

1. Annuals live for only one year. During this time they germinate, grow, flower and

How a young herbaceous stem starts to turn into a woody trunk

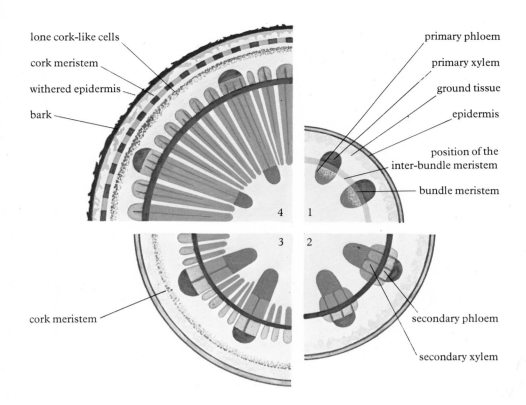

lone cork-like cells
cork meristem
withered epidermis
bark

cork meristem

primary phloem
primary xylem
ground tissue
epidermis
position of the inter-bundle meristem
bundle meristem

secondary phloem

secondary xylem

Sector 1 The young stem consists of an outer protective coat (the epidermis) which encloses a living ground tissue through which vascular bundles conduct water (via the red xylem) and sugar and other manufactured substances (via the green phloem) around the plant. As the plant grows taller the stem starts to get top heavy and extra strengthening material is required.

Sector 2 A new (secondary) meristem, the inter-bundle cambium, appears and starts to divide producing secondary phloem and secondary xylem (wood), enough to support the growing plant and keep its parts well supplied with everything they need.

Sector 3 As growth continues the outer layers come under more and more strain until eventually the protective epidermis must rupture. Before this happens another secondary meristem develops within the stem.

Sector 4 This is the cork cambium or phellogen and it divides to produce a new complex protective coat called cork. The old epidermis is now dead and slowly decays away. As the secondary wood develops, the transverse medullary rays elongate. Their function is to transport material from the side to the middle and vice versa.

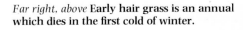

Above **Monocot leaves are often narrow and have parallel veins.**

Above **Dicot leaves are often broad and have reticulate veins.**

set seeds to provide next year's generation of plants.

2. Biennials live for two years. In the first year they germinate and grow, building up a food store in tap-roots. In the second year they use up this store in a burst of flowering and seed production before dying.

3. Perennials live for several years at least and generally flower each year. They over-winter in a state of dormancy before beginning to grow again in spring.

Far right, above **Early hair grass is an annual which dies in the first cold of winter.**

Far right, below **Nettle is a perennial which grows new shoots each year.**

Right **Wild carrot is a biennial. The tap root stores food from the first year for use in the second.**

Reproduction

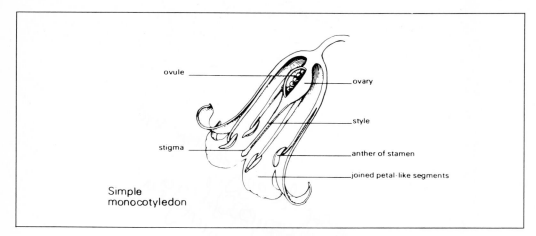

Simple monocotyledon

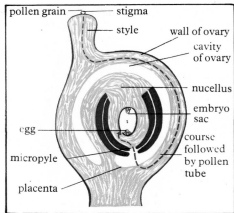

There is amazing variety to be found in the colour, shape and structure of flowers, but they all have the same purpose — to bring about reproduction.

Plants produce male and female cells in their flowers. The male cells are contained in pollen, which develop in the anthers. The female cells develop in ovules contained within the ovary. Above the ovary is a region called the style, terminated by a stigma, the receptive part of the organ. The transfer of pollen from the anthers to the stigma is called pollination.

Sometimes the male and female cells are produced in different flowers or even in different plants, but more commonly both are found in the same flower. In this case there is usually some mechanism or device to prevent pollen being deposited on the stigma of the same flower.

When a suitable pollen grain lands on the stigma it produces a pollen tube which grows down into the ovary. When it reaches an ovule it enters by means of a tiny opening called the micropyle. Two cells are then released from the pollen tube, one of which fuses with the egg cell to form the embryo plant; the other fuses with different cells to form food tissues for the developing plant.

After fertilization various changes occur in the flower. The outer walls of the ovules harden to form the seed coat, the ovary wall develops into the wall of the fruit and the petals wither and die. An ovary may contain just a single ovule or many; each one successfully fertilized will develop into a seed.

Plants can reproduce themselves without the necessity of producing seeds by vegetative or asexual reproduction. The offspring will be identical to their parents and in some instances this is particularly desirable, for example cultivated plants where a gardener wishes to conserve certain characteristics of the parent plant.

The ways plants have of reproducing vegetatively are many and varied. Some plants such as the blackberry and the raspberry produce suckers from their roots which give rise to new plants. The grasses will often colonize large areas by producing new shoots from underground stems or rhizomes. Some plants even have reproductive leaves; for example, the indoor house plant *Kalanchoë*, whose common name 'mother-of-thousands' refers to the numerous tiny plants that arise in the notches along the leaf margins. These drop off and fall into the soil where they take root, providing the main means of propagation for this plant.

Some plants have seeds that are reproduced asexually. Violets, for example, bear some flowers that are much smaller than the rest and never open. Seeds that come from these flowers are genetically identical to the parent. The larger flowers are pollinated by insects and produce seeds in the normal way.

Above, left **Cross-section through a monocot flower.**

Above **Diagram to show the path followed by the pollen tube.**

Left **The roots of the creeping thistle (*Irsium arvense*) spread through the soil and every so often send up a new plant, making this a difficult weed to eradicate.**

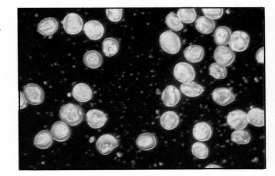

*Above, left **Kalanchoë daigremontianum** produces large numbers of small plantlets along its leaf margins.*

Above The sweet violet sends runners over the ground with plantlets at the end. The offspring may remain attached to the parent for some time until the runners eventually decay. Another plant which reproduces this way is the strawberry.

Right Pollen grains magnified to show their air sacs which aid dispersal.

Opposite, far left Blackberries are propagated commercially by cuttings planted in late summer. They will begin to show new growth the following spring.

Opposite, left A new shoot arises from the base of a blackberry. It may eventually arch over and take root.

Pollinators

Above **The stamens of grasses hang down on long slender filaments to catch the wind.**

Below **Purplish lines on the petals of eyebright act as honey guides, indicating to insects where the nectaries will be found.**

Above **Bird-pollinated flowers produce copious supplies of watery nectar to attract their visitors.**

Since land plants are stationary organisms without the ability to move from place to place, they need the assistance of outside agents to carry their pollen to the female eggcells. With some plants this agent is the wind, but for this method to be successful, vast quantities of pollen must be produced in order to increase the chances of pollen reaching a suitable plant of the same species. The grasses are wind pollinated and have long, feathery stigmas to catch the windblown pollen.

Insect-pollinated plants must have some way of attracting their visitors, and usually this takes the form of brightly coloured petals, scent and a food source, either in the form of the pollen itself or nectar, a sugary fluid secreted from special glands which is very attractive to insects.

There is no guarantee that an insect visitor will visit another plant of the same species to effect cross-pollination; however, many plants evolved flowers adapted to attract only one or a few kinds of insect. In this way the chances of that insect visiting another of the same kind are considerably increased.

The many different types of bees are an important group of pollinators and the flowers they visit often have a distinctive colour and pattern to attract them. Some flowers have honey guides which indicate to the insect where the nectar will be found. These markings are often invisible to the human eye but the eyes of the bee, which are sensitive to a slightly different spectrum of light, can detect them. A photograph taken with ultraviolet light renders them visible.

Flowers that are pollinated by night-flying moths are typically white or pale coloured so that they stand out well in the dark, and they usually emit a strong scent at night when the moths are about. The evening primrose (*Oenothera*) and the South American yucca are both pollinated by moths. The yucca is so dependent upon a single species of moth to pollinate its flowers that it always fails to set fruit when grown in cultivation away from its natural habitat where the moth lives.

Hummingbirds are the most important group of birds that regularly visit flowers and pollinate them. Birds have a poorly developed sense of smell and so these flowers usually have little or no scent. Birds are, however, attracted by colour, especially red, and consequently this is the predominant colour of bird-pollinated flowers, with yellow the second most common colour. These flowers all produce large amounts of nectar to attract birds, but to discourage insects from feeding there they have tended to evolve long, tubular flowers, the bottom of which insects cannot reach.

In the tropical areas of both the Old World and the New World, flower-visiting bats occur. In many respects these flowers are similar to those pollinated by birds, being large and producing much nectar; however, they are not usually brightly coloured and frequently emit a musty, fruit-like odour to attract the bats, who carry the pollen from flower to flower on their fur.

Left, top **The pyrethrum makes its small flowers more conspicuous by clustering many together into a single head. Insects may pollinate many flowers during a visit.**

Left **This Peruvian butterfly settling on a flower to feed will carry pollen to the next bloom it visits.**

Below, left **All these flowers are members of the same plant family *Polemonaceae*, each adapted to attract different pollinators.**

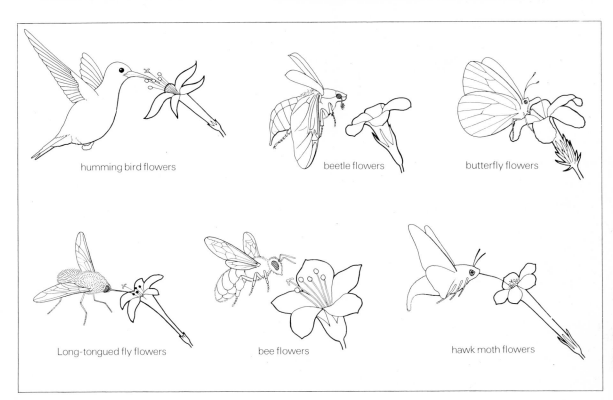

humming bird flowers

beetle flowers

butterfly flowers

Long-tongued fly flowers

bee flowers

hawk moth flowers

Below **Blue delphiniums are pollinated by bees, while red ones are pollinated by humming birds.**

Dispersal

Birds are not the only creatures to feed on the brightly coloured berries of plants and aid their dispersal. Here, a dormouse is attracted by the berries of hawthorn.

Above **Tumbleweeds collect along a fence in western Texas, U.S.A.**

Below **These dandelion 'parachutes' will soon be blown away in the wind.**

Plants have evolved many different ways of ensuring that their seeds are dispersed a good distance from the parent plant. This helps to prevent overcrowding and competition from the offspring for available light and water and, more importantly, enables a species to colonize new areas and increase its distribution.

The simplest form of dispersal does not rely on seeds, but occurs by fragmentation. This method is particularly common among water plants, for example the Canadian pondweed (*Elodea canadensis*), where pieces of stem become detached, float away and continue growing.

However, the majority of flowering plants use seeds as their main means of dispersal. In some cases it is the seed alone that is scattered; in others it is the fruit, containing the seeds, that is adapted for dispersal.

Many plants rely on agents such as wind, water, animals or birds to disperse their seeds for them. For wind-dispersed seeds it is an advantage to be very light so they may be carried a long distance. The seeds of orchids are among the tiniest and are carried in the wind like dust. Larger seeds usually have some kind of appendage to help them float, such as a wing or feathery hairs. Many members of the Compositae family have a 'parachute' made up of fine hairs; seeds of the willowherbs (*Epilobium* spp.) and *Clematis* have plumed hairs attached.

Sometimes it is not just the seeds that are dispersed, but the whole plant takes off, as is the case with *Amaranthus graecizans*. These are known as tumbleweeds and either the complete plant, or the seed-bearing portion, breaks off and is blown along the ground by the wind, scattering seeds as it goes.

Some seeds have a fleshy appendage called an aril that is brightly coloured and aimed at attracting animals and birds. More commonly, the seed is completely enclosed within a fleshy fruit which changes colour as the seeds ripen. Unripe fruits are usually green to render them inconspicuous amongst the green leaves. Also, during this time they often have an unpleasant taste to discourage animals from eating them before the seeds have ripened. The change in colour that occurs when the seeds are mature indicates that the fruit is ready to be eaten. The animal either discards the seeds or they pass through its body unharmed, and indeed some seeds will not germinate unless they have done so.

A number of other plants have fruits or seeds which become attached to the fur of animals or the feathers of birds by means of spines, hooks and barbs. In this way they may be transported huge distances.

The common gorse (*Ulex europaeus*) and the Himalayan balsam (*Impatiens glandulifera*) both have explosive seed pods. As the seeds mature internal tensions build up in the walls of the pod and one day the slightest movement triggers them to burst open, scattering their seeds as they do so.

Above **The hooked bracts surrounding the flowers of burdock readily become attached to fur and clothing.**

Above **The flowers of ivy-leaved toadflax initially face outwards to attract insects, but after fertilisation the flower stalks curve back to position the developing capsules in small nooks and crevices in the wall on which it grows. This ensures the seeds are deposited in a suitable habitat.**

Below **The fruits of goosegrass are covered with many tiny hooked spines which stick on to passing animals.**

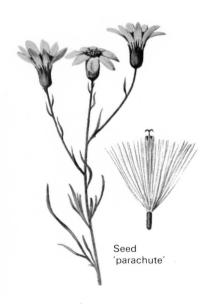

Seed 'parachute'

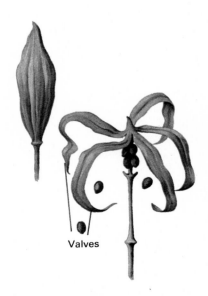

Valves

Above **Senecio douglasii** **is one of many** **Compositae** **whose seeds have a parachute of fine hairs attached.**

Right **The violent rupturing of the balsam capsule causes the seeds to be ejected a considerable distance.**

15

Tundra

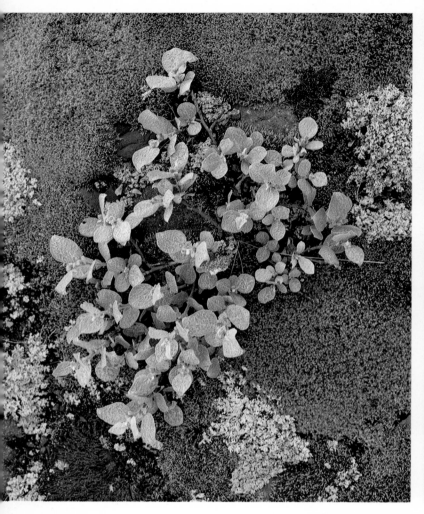

The area known as tundra is a vast barren-looking plain, occasionally interrupted by small lakes and morasses, that lies in the arctic regions of northern Russia and northern North America. It is an area little influenced by man, being only sparsely inhabited by Lapps, Samoyeds and Eskimos who live a nomadic way of life, hunting and fishing for their food and clothes. In the Southern Hemisphere tundra vegetation is found in many areas of the maritime Antarctic.

The most conspicuous feature of the tundra vegetation is the complete absence of any trees. The only plants to be seen for mile upon mile are small herbs and low-growing shrubs, such as dwarf willows (*Salix* spp.) and birches (*Betula* spp.) that grow close to the ground where the effects of the strong winds that sweep the tundra are minimized. A mature flowering plant of a willow such as the common *Salix arctica* may be barely 15cm across. In places there are no flowering plants at all, only a covering of mosses and lichens.

Tundra regions are characterized by the permafrost layer, a zone of the underlying soil that is permanently frozen throughout the year. Its thickness varies, but it may be several metres thick in places. During the summer the upper layers melt, forming bogs in places because the still-frozen soil beneath prevents the water draining away.

Another characteristic of the tundra is the short, cool summer which gives the plants a

growing season of only sixty to a hundred days per year. In order to make full use of the time available for growth the plants must rapidly become active as soon as the conditions are suitable. Many do this by utilizing their extensive food reserves which are stored in underground organs such as rhizomes. Nearly all tundra plants are perennials; annuals can only survive in the most favourable situations and they remain very small.

Above, left **Salix lanata grows close to the ground in Iceland where there is less disturbance from the strong winds.**

Above **The lovely arctic poppy has flowers ranging in size from 2 − 5cm across and attracts many insects.**

Some perennials produce flowers in one year that remain in bud and unopened. The buds of *Ranunculus nivalis*, the snow buttercup, pass the winter in this stage and the following season, as soon as the snows melt, begin to flower, a long time before other plants have even begun to produce new growth. The purple saxifrage (*Saxifraga oppositiflora*) also forms its flowers in this way and can be seen in full flower within a week of snow melt.

The flowers of tundra plants are often large in proportion to the size of the plant and brightly coloured to attract insects who effect their pollination. The lovely arctic poppy (*Papaver radicatum*) is one of several tundra plants that has a flower which acts as a kind of parabolic reflector, trapping heat from the sun so that the temperature around its reproductive organs is several degrees warmer than the surrounding air. The warmth encourages insects to settle on the flower, transferring pollen when they do so.

Despite the various ways tundra plants have of attracting insects to pollinate their flowers, the majority rely heavily on vegetative reproduction because the chances of seedlings becoming successfully established are very small.

Above **Permafrost is usually hidden from view, but here the ground has been eroded away by a stream, revealing the thick layers of ice below.**

Below, left **Purple saxifrage.**

Below **Richardson's saxifrage.**

Alpines

The alpine zone of a mountain is one of the harshest places to live, but plants do grow there. In summer these so-called alpines can transform a mountain from a dreary rock-littered place to a scene of incredible beauty, full of brightly coloured flowers.

The summer is short, however, and alpines must produce their flowers at the first opportunity in an effort to ensure that they are successfully pollinated and seeds produced before the first snows of winter arrive.

Some plants by-pass the need to produce seeds and instead exhibit a phenomenon known as vivipary, whereby fully formed plantlets are created where the flowers would have been. The alpine meadow grass (*Poa alpina*) is one of several grasses that frequently has miniature plants formed in the upper parts of its spikelets, each with tiny leaves and partly developed roots, all ready to grow the moment it falls to the ground.

During the long winter growth is impossible for alpines and they remain dormant under a covering of snow which insulates and protects them against the extreme temperatures. In the Andes some of the plants may stay covered by snow for several years, remaining dormant until the snow begins to melt.

Alpines usually have an extensive root system to anchor them firmly in the substrate. This is particularly important in areas of scree where the small stones are continually moving downwards. Long roots are also important in obtaining adequate water. A tiny alpine a few centimetres high is quite likely to have roots a metre or more in length.

Obtaining sufficient water is a big problem for these plants because it is either frozen and falls as snow or else it quickly drains away through the thin mountain soils. The leaves are often adapted to reduce water loss by having a waxy covering or a layer or woolly hairs. The hairs also benefit the plant by maintaining a layer of warmth around the plant.

The cushion-forming alpines have another way of conserving warmth. Their leaves are very small and grow tightly packed together forming a heat trap. Small insects often take advantage of this fact and visit the plants to keep warm, pollinating the flowers as they do so. The low growth habit of these and other alpines also serves to protect them from the strong mountain winds.

Although the typical alpine is a dwarf, cushion or rosette-forming plant that hugs the ground for protection, by no means all alpines have adopted such precautions. Many, such as the alpine columbine (*Aquilegia alpina*) are ordinary herbaceous plants. However, they do tend to grow in more protected locations, taking full advantage of local micro-climates such as occur on the sheltered sides of a boulder.

Left **Gentiana ornata.**

Above **Autumn gentian *Gentianella amarella*.**

Opposite, bottom left The rosette habit is very common among alpine plants.

Above Alpine lady's mantle grows among other alpine plants on a small rocky ledge.

Below The dwarf snowbell (**Soldanella alpina**) is another member of the primrose family.

Opposite, bottom right The thick covering of matted hairs on the edelweiss provide insulation against the cold.

Below, left **Primula rubra**, one of the many lovely alpine plants that is sought after by gardeners for planting in rockeries.

Mountains

The types of plants found on mountains can be divided into several vegetation zones, though they vary to a certain extent with the height of the particular mountain and with the area of the world in which it occurs. There are many complex factors affecting the plants, but one of the main reasons why the changes in vegetation occur is because of the variations in temperature experienced at the different altitudes. On average, the temperature will fall by 0·5°C for every 100m climbed.

Plants are also affected by the steepness of the mountain sides because the angle the sun shines on the ground affects how much heat the ground will absorb. South-facing slopes are usually the warmest in the Northern Hemisphere, but in the Southern Hemisphere the situation is reversed.

Other factors also to be considered are the increased intensity of radiation occurring at

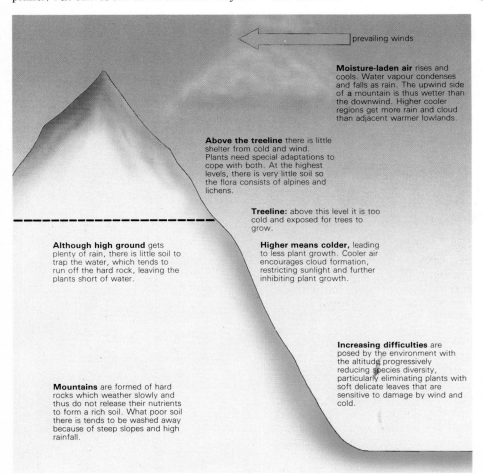

prevailing winds

Moisture-laden air rises and cools. Water vapour condenses and falls as rain. The upwind side of a mountain is thus wetter than the downwind. Higher cooler regions get more rain and cloud than adjacent warmer lowlands.

Above the treeline there is little shelter from cold and wind. Plants need special adaptations to cope with both. At the highest levels, there is very little soil so the flora consists of alpines and lichens.

Treeline: above this level it is too cold and exposed for trees to grow.

Although high ground gets plenty of rain, there is little soil to trap the water, which tends to run off the hard rock, leaving the plants short of water.

Higher means colder, leading to less plant growth. Cooler air encourages cloud formation, restricting sunlight and further inhibiting plant growth.

Increasing difficulties are posed by the environment with the altitude progressively reducing species diversity, particularly eliminating plants with soft delicate leaves that are sensitive to damage by wind and cold.

Mountains are formed of hard rocks which weather slowly and thus do not release their nutrients to form a rich soil. What poor soil there is tends to be washed away because of steep slopes and high rainfall.

Left **The upland environment.**

Below **Distribution of the world's major mountain chains. Those formed during the Cainozoic era are the most recent in origin.**

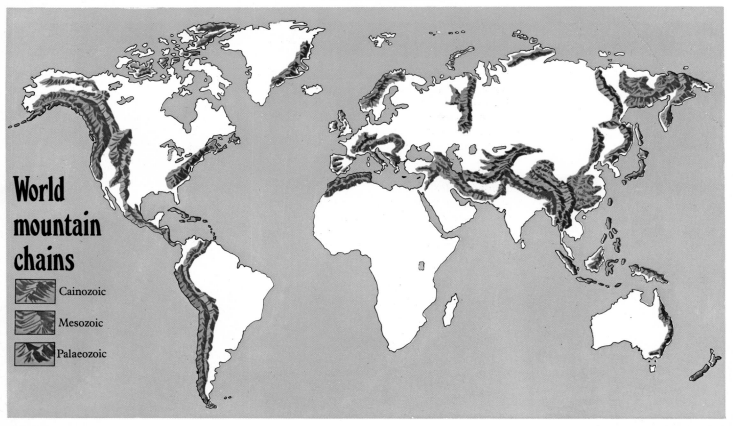

World mountain chains

Cainozoic

Mesozoic

Palaeozoic

Crops grown
in Andes

Above 2000 metres
Grassland, cold
Crop: wheat
Livestock: sheep, llamas

1000 to 2000 metres
Fewer trees, cooler
Crops: coffee, maize

Sea-level to 1000 metres
Forest, warm
Crops: cocoa, bananas, sugar-cane

Above **Cattle graze on the rich alpine pastures during the summer months.**

higher altitudes as well as the greater wind speeds experienced.

The typical zones on a mountain are, starting from the bottom, montane, sub-alpine and alpine. However, it is not always possible to distinguish clearly between them and the height at which they develop varies with local conditions and latitude.

The montane zone is typically occupied by woodlands, though in some areas this is replaced by shrub or grassland if it is an area of low rainfall. In tropical areas trees are able to grow at far higher altitudes than in temperate regions because of the increased moisture levels.

In the subalpine zone trees still occur but they become increasingly sparse towards the upper limits of this zone. The climate is cooler and drier. Grasses and other herbaceous plants are often the dominant vegetation and a typical feature of this zone is the lush meadowland containing a rich variety of plantlife. The meadows are economically important too, because they provide a rich summer pasture for cattle, and hay for the winter. However, they only develop in the wetter areas; where the rainfall is reduced a ground cover of heathers (*Erica* spp.), together with other members of this family, predominates.

The highest part of the mountain, where the alpine zone occurs, is characterized by plants which are specialized to survive in a rigorous environment. They have many problems to overcome, such as thin soils, water shortages, strong winds and a short growing season. They show many similarities to plants of the tundra; however, the flora of the alpine zone is much richer than that of the tundra.

Although most plants of the alpine zone are adapted to survive in dry conditions, in places where snow meltwater collects and cannot readily escape, small peat bogs develop in which sedges (*Carex* spp.) and cotton grasses (*Eriophorum* spp.) can be seen.

Right **Some of the many grasses and sedges occurring in mountain districts. Often they form the dominant vegetation over large areas of upland.**

21

Giant Senecios and Lobelias

Above **Mount Kenya in East Africa, where both the giant senecios and lobelias occur, reaches over 500 metres high.**

In equatorial East Africa there are high mountains, known as the legendary Mountains of the Moon, where from month to month the temperature is much the same so there are no distinct seasons, though there are great fluctuations between the day- and night-time temperatures. It is a desolate area, a land of damp, acid soils over which cold, wet winds gust for much of the year. During the day it may be hot and sunny but the nights are invariably cold and snow is frequent.

On other high mountains such harsh conditions produce low-growing, dwarf plants that hug the ground for protection, but here in the African mountains, rising high on the equator, grow extraordinary tall plants – gigantic senecios and lobelias that have become inexplicably large, some of them attaining a height of six metres when in flower.

Each mountain area has a characteristic variety of lobelia and the variation in the shape and hairiness of the floral bracts is used to distinguish between them. The blue-flowered *Lobelia telekii* grows on Mount Elgon and is pollinated by sunbirds who perch on

the woolly bracts to seek out the nectar of the flowers nestling in between.

Lobelia deckeni can only be seen on Kilimanjaro in Tanzania where it is often found growing alongside some of the species of giant senecios. It is hard to believe that these huge, tree-like senecios are close relatives of the small, yellow-flowered groundsel that is a common weed of temperate regions.

Both the giant senecios and giant lobelias have leaves which protect the stems and shoots from the bitter cold at night. The lower leaves may be dead but they usually remain attached to the stems and hang upside down to provide protection. The upper leaves fold up at night to protect the young shoots. As morning comes and the air temperature starts to rise they slowly unfold again.

Senecio brassica from Mount Kenya has a thick felty covering on the undersurface of its leaves which provides efficient insulation for the shoots when the leaves are folded up during the night. It has been recorded that, whilst the outside temperature is a cold −3·9°C (25°F), the shoots may have a temperature of 1·7°C (35°F).

Below **The common groundsel, usually less than 30cm high, is a close relative of the giant African senecios.**

Right **Lobelia telekii** on Mount Kenya.
Below **Senecio johnstoni** at about 4000 metres on the slopes of Mount Elgon, Uganda.

23

Poppies

The Papaveraceae or poppy family is a widespread and successful group of plants, occurring throughout most temperate parts of the Northern Hemisphere and a few parts of the Southern. They occupy a wide range of habitats, from high mountains to shingle coasts and arable land to semi-desert. Many are species which favour disturbed ground and these have taken advantage of cultivation to extend their ranges and become common. Poppies have a high reproductive rate. A field poppy may produce up to 400 flowers and 20 000 seeds in a single season! With such capabilities they have few problems maintaining population levels. The seeds can lie dormant in the soil for many years so that when it is disturbed again by ploughing a whole new 'crop' springs up.

Most Papaveraceae have large, showy, four-petalled flowers in a range of vivid colours. The field poppy, *Papaver rhoeas*, is one of the few truly red flowers found in Europe. The horned poppy, *Glaucium flavum*, has shiny yellow flowers while the Californian poppy, *Escholtzia californica*, ranges in colour from white through to scarlet.

The Himalayan poppies of the genus *Mecanopsis* can be yellow or red, but the best known species have flowers of a deep, rich blue. *Mecanopsis* is confined to the Himalayas and W. China except for one species, *Mecanopsis cambrica*, the Welsh poppy. It is

Left **California poppies cover this grassy area with a blaze of yellow and orange flowers.**

this poppy which grows in western Europe.

Two unusual poppy genera are *Macleaya* and *Bocconia* which are apetalous — their flowers completely lack petals and are grouped into dense, plume-like clusters. Bocconias actually form small trees.

A feature shared by all members of the family is the production of sticky, latex-like sap. This is usually white, although that of the horned poppy is orange. Latex obtained from the opium poppy is the basis of a large drug industry.

Opposite, top left **Himalayan poppies, such as *Mecanopsis horridula* are famous for their striking blue flowers.**

Opposite, top right **The flower heads of *Macleaya microcarpa* have earned it the name plume poppy.**

Opposite, bottom right **A field of drug-producing white opium poppies (*Papaver somniferum*) in Thailand.**

Above left **The mauve form of opium poppy (subspecies *hortense*) yields a useful oil, but no drug.**

Above, right **The edge of this cornfield has been colonised by poppies.**

Opium poppies

The source of the powerful drug opium is the opium poppy, *Papaver somniferum*. Opium growers use a special knife to make a series of incisions in the unripe seed capsule. The cuts weep a sticky latex which is collected, dried and rolled into balls of raw opium. Raw opium can be used as a drug but it is usually refined to extract the numerous alkaloid chemicals which are the basis of its pharmaecutical properties. Opium derivatives include morphine, codeine and heroin, all powerful narcotics. Despite its increasing criminal associations, opium and its products are valuable medicines.

Opium poppies are tall plants with slightly bluish leaves and large white, pink or purple flowers with distinctive dark centres. Although it probably originated in Turkey, the opium poppy is now widely grown in the Balkan peninsula, the Middle East, India and China. The notorious 'golden triangle' of Southeast Asia is a major growing region.

Papaver somniferum has two subspecies but only one, subspecies *somniferum*, yields the drug. The other, subspecies *hortense*, is a popular and innocuous garden plant. Only the latex of the seed capsule is narcotic. The seeds, which yield a useful oil, are widely used in baking.

Heathlands

The oceanic belts bordering the Atlantic Ocean and the North Sea in Europe and the northern coasts of North America support a characteristic heathland vegetation. Similar regions occur in the Southern Hemisphere, for example in southern South America. Heaths are areas generally lacking tall trees and shrubs but dominated by small ericoid shrubs. Despite the mild oceanic influences, heathlands are harsh habitats. They are usually quite exposed places and the soils are always acid, even when they overlie basic (i.e. alkaline) rocks. This is because they

contain layers of peat — vegetable matter which has not fully decomposed. Peat makes a soil acidic and poor, low in minerals and badly aerated. Where rainfall is high or drainage poor, wet heaths, more usually known as moors, occur. There is little difference between heaths and moors, one type grading into the other, but generally heaths are dry and moors are wet.

The dominant shrubs are characteristically dwarf and much-branched with tiny, evergreen leaves. They are referred to as ericoids because these features are exempli-

fied by members of the heather family, the Ericaceae. Indeed all the Northern Hemisphere heaths are found within the distribution range of heather or ling (*Calluna vulgaris*), which is the dominant plant in all but the wettest and most exposed sites. Other prominent members of the family are the heaths and bell-heathers (*Erica* species) in wetter areas and bilberries (*Vaccinium* species) on exposed summits.

Not all ericoids belong to the Ericaceae however. The crowberries (*Empetrum* species), for example, closely resemble the

Left **Heather flowers prolifically and can turn whole hillsides purple with its blossom.**

Below **Another common moorland plant is harebell,** *Campanula rotundifolia*

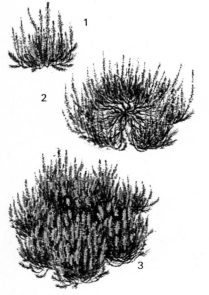

Far left **Heather has a cyclic growth pattern. Young plants are compact bushes. As they age they die back in the centre, while the outer branches take root, forming a ring of new young plants round the centre of the old one.**

Left **The lichen** *Cladonia coccifera* **is often found growing beneath heather, especially in the centre of old plants which are dying back.**

Above **Sphagnum squarrosum** and the more delicate **Sphagnum fimbriatum**. This moss has a great capacity for holding water and can be wrung out like a sponge. It is one of the main constituents of peat.

Below Large areas of sphagnum may form blanket bogs – very wet areas which support plants such as cotton grasses.

Ericaceae in appearance but belong to the Empetraceae. They are particularly important in Southern Hemisphere heaths. The heathland shrubs provide a protective canopy for a number of other plants, especially lichens.

When the peat is very wet and boggy a very different vegetation is found. Bogs are frequently dominated by sphagnum moss and the white fluffy seed-heads of cotton grass (*Eriophorum* species), relatives of the sedges which have rhizomes specially adapted to grow in waterlogged, poorly aerated soils. Conditions here are very poor indeed and plants must take advantage of any chance to bolster their supply of minerals, especially nitrogen compounds. Carnivorous plants such as sundews and bladderworts abound in these places. Their unique lifestyle allows them to survive by using insects, which they trap and digest, as an additional source of food.

In suitable conditions heathlands can replace forests when the latter are cleared, and many heaths have been extended in this way. Heather moors provide good grazing for hardy hill breeds and, in Scotland, for the Red Grouse. Once established, they are often maintained for this purpose. As they age heather plants produce more wood and fewer young shoots, providing less grazing. To prevent this and keep the plants in an

Above Bilberries often grow among heather. On more exposed sites they may become dominant, forming 'bilberry summits' or 'bilberry moors'.

actively gowing phase they are regularly burnt. The interval between burnings is about ten years. If the plants are left longer they lose the ability to regenerate easily. Regular maintenance of this kind produces almost pure stands of heather.

Carnivorous Plants

Tales of amazing man-eating plants from far-away places have always turned out to be just fantasy, but there are plants which trap and digest small animals, mostly insects—the carnivorous plants.

Green plants obtain most of the substances they require for healthy growth from sunlight, oxygen and carbon dioxide by the process of photosynthesis, whereby simple chemicals are built into the more complex carbohydrates which provide energy sources and a base for synthesizing numerous other chemicals needed by the plant.

However there are minerals such as potassium, calcium, iron and nitrogen compounds, among others, which a plant cannot synthesize itself and must obtain by absorption from the soil.

Some areas are very deficient in minerals; habitats such as acid-bogs, marshes and swamps are often particularly mineral poor. The carnivorous plants are well-adapted to live in such environments because they have evolved the means of capturing small

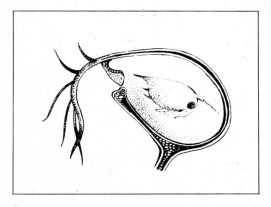

creatures to provide them with the substances they require.

Plants are, of course, unable to go off and hunt their prey, so they must lure the visitors to them, which they do by a variety of different trapping mechanisms.

The traps of carnivorous plants are leaves which have become highly modified, often scarcely resembling leaves at all, and can be mistaken instead for the flowers. Some have

Above **Venus flytrap. An insect stimulating one of the three sensitive hairs on the upper lid will cause the trap to shut.**

Left **The underwater trap of a bladderwort.**

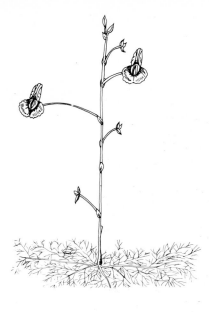

stimulated by prey such as water fleas and mosquito larvae, cause the door to open and with an inrush of water the prey is swept inside, the door closing promptly behind.

The pitcher plants have passive traps. They belong to three different plant families, the Sarraceniaceae from North America, the Nepenthaceae mainly from tropical Asia, and the Cephalotaceae from Western Australia. Their pitchers show slight differences in structure, but they all have the same function.

The pitchers of *Nepenthes* are produced at the end of slender tendrils which arise from the leaves. They vary in size from a few centimetres to a foot in length, and are often brightly coloured with reds and purples to make them conspicuous and attract insect visitors. Inside the pitcher entrance are smooth waxy cells which make the surface so slippery that insects alighting there fall down into the body of the pitcher where they drown in the mixture of water and digestive enzyme that is contained there.

Below, left **Nepenthes alba. The projecting lid over the pitcher protects it from heavy rain.**

Below **Sarracenia pupurea, whose pitchers may reach 46cm in length.**

Above **The flowers of bladderwort are raised well above the water surface to attract insect pollinators.**

Opposite, bottom **The sundew is seen here growing with another carnivorous plant, the butterwort. Its leaves are covered in sticky reddish hairs. Insects touching these hairs are held fast and the leaf slowly curls over th enclose them.**

active traps where the prey is captured in a rapid movement by the plant. A well-known plant with this kind of trap is Venus flytrap (*Dionaea muscipula*), quite localized in its native habitat in the south-eastern United States but now widely sold for cultivation.

The trap resembles a bivalved shell, fringed with spine-like hairs, the two halves coming together to entrap the prey.

A different kind of active trap is demonstrated by the bladderworts (*Utricularia* spp.) which are small aquatic plants. They have an underwater trap with a small flap-like door at one end. Near the entrance are sensitive trigger hairs which, when

Tropical Rain Forests

Above **Only a hundredth of the sunlight reaching the rain forest filters down through the closed canopy of trees to reach the sparse vegetation growing below.**

Left **The world's remaining tropical forests, rich in plant and animal life, are being destroyed at an alarming rate.**

Opposite, bottom left **Coelogyne massangeana is one of the many species of orchid which grow epiphytically on the forest trees.**

Evergreen tropical rain forests occur in parts of Central and South America, Africa and South-east Asia, growing in lowland areas where there is a hot climate and a substantial and well-distributed rainfall. They are characterized by the many lianes, climbing plants and epiphytes that grow there.

Trees are the dominant plants of the rain forest community, their crowns, with the branches often interlocking, form a more or less unbroken canopy that casts shade on all below. Beneath the main canopy smaller trees grow, preventing even more light from reaching the ground. This lack of sunlight on the forest floor results in a very sparse undergrowth, comprising mainly seedlings and saplings of the forest trees, with only a handful of herbaceous plants that can survive in such a dim environment, scattered around.

It is only in clearings, along river banks or at higher altitudes where the tree cover is less thick and light can penetrate that we find the dense and in places almost impenetrable ground vegetation that many imagine is typical.

If the forest floor has a somewhat sparse flora, the plant life in the tree-tops compensates. Here, high up in the forest canopy, live the epiphytes, growing on trunks, branches and even the still-living leaves of trees. Many different kinds of plants have adopted this way of life. Non-flowering plants such as algae, mosses, liverworts, lichens and ferns are commonly epiphytic; but most lovely are the exotic and sometimes bizarre flowering plants, providing colour in the trees which themselves usually have inconspicuous greenish or whitish flowers. Large numbers of orchids and bromeliads abound, perched high in the upper canopies of the forest.

They are not parasites of the trees, for many of them can grow successfully on the ground given the right conditions; they just use the trees for support.

The epiphytic way of life is a highly specialized one. They have overcome the difficulty of reaching the light, but their aerial habitat brings a new set of problems, the most important of which are water supply and lack of soil. Although they live in a very wet environment, epiphytes frequently suffer a water shortage and so they exhibit many of the adaptations more commonly associated with desert plants, such as thick fleshy leaves for storing water. The roots are covered with a tough waterproof layer called the velamen which prevents water loss by evaporation. However, so the plant can take in water, this covering is absent from areas where the roots touch the support.

Right, above **Phalaenopsis schillerana** from the **Philippines.**

Right, below **Cattleya bowringiana** from Central **America.**

Bromeliads

Bromeliads are very distinctive tropical plants belonging to the family *Bromeliaceae*. They are native to an area stretching from the southern United States of America down to Chile, with the greatest diversity occurring in Brazil. A single species occurs in West Africa.

Numerous species are grown as house plants for their attractive foliage or striking inflorescences. However, the most widely cultivated plant of this family is the pineapple (*Ananas comosus*) which, with its large number of cultivars, is extensively grown for its fruit and has become naturalized in many areas.

The largest bromeliads, called puyas, grow in South America. Their long, narrow, dagger-like leaves often bear sharp spines along the edge. *Puya raimondii* from the mountains of Peru blooms only once in its life, but when it does it is spectacular, producing a tall inflorescence bearing many thousands of greenish-white flowers. Once the millions of tiny winged seeds have been dispersed the plant dies away completely. It has been estimated that *Puya raimondii* may grow for as long as sixty years before flowering.

Many bromeliads are epiphytes, exhibiting a great diversity in form. The widely distributed Spanish moss (*Tillandsia usneoides*) that hangs down from trees and even telegraph wires in long festoons of twisted strands, can survive in very dry habitats. Except when young it has no roots, but absorbs water through special scales on the leaf-surface called trichomes, which give the leaves a greyish appearance. During wet weather the trichomes soak up moisture like blotting paper and the water transfers into the leaf tissues where it can be stored.

Spanish moss often reproduces vegetatively by pieces of stem breaking off and rooting. Birds often help the plants in this way by pulling off strands to use in building their nests.

The 'tank' bromeliads are mostly epiphytic, growing on trees and cliff-sides. They have few roots, but their leaves overlap at the base to form reservoirs or tanks for collecting and storing rain water as a precaution against times of shortage. Some species with large rosettes of leaves can hold as much as five litres (more than a gallon) of water. Most tank bromeliads harbour an interesting flora and fauna within their leaf rosettes. Mosquito larvae, aquatic insects and frogs live and breed alongside algae and small flowering plants. In the humus that collects above the water level salamanders, lizards and tree snakes can be found.

Above **The spectacular *Puya raimondii* in flower.**

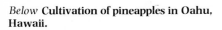
Below **Cultivation of pineapples in Oahu, Hawaii.**

Below **Pineapples are not only cultivated for their fruit. This variegated form has attractively striped leaves.**

Above This bromeliad has not yet flowered, but the brightly coloured leaf-bases provide an attractive display.

Below The large-flowered *Billbergia* is an epiphyte whilst the smaller-flowered *Cryptanthus*, popularly known as an earth-star, prefers to grow flat against rocks.

Above Spanish moss is widespread in tropical America and the West Indies.

Below Two epiphytic bromeliads continue to flower after their perch has fallen.

Aroids

Below The large, shiny spathes of ***Anthurium andreanum*** come in a variety of colours, from white through to pink and scarlet. It is popularly known as the flamingo plant.

Above ***Lysichitum americanum*** is native to north-west America, where it grows in boggy areas. The leaves, almost a metre long, are produced after the flowers have already appeared.

Opposite, bottom The Swiss cheese plant from Mexico makes an excellent indoor pot plant.

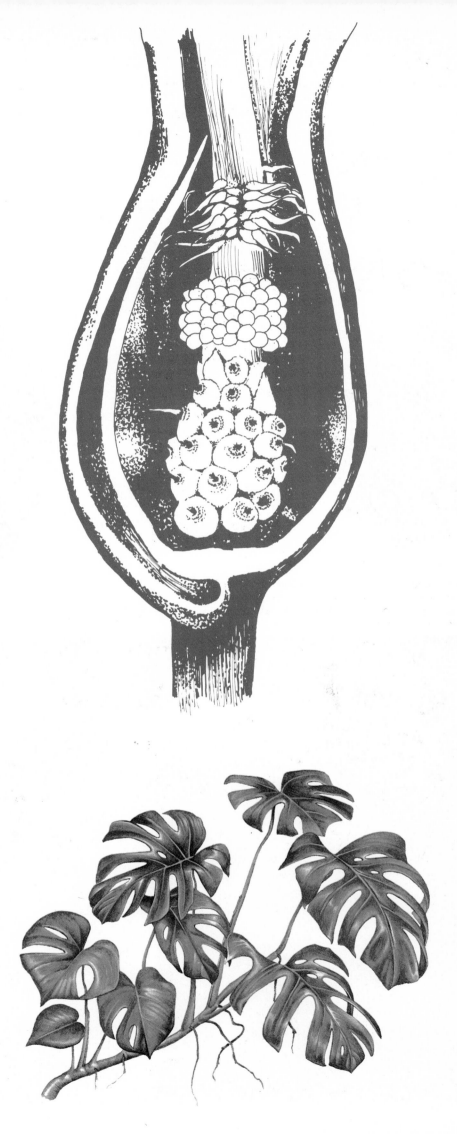

The aroids, members of the *Araceae* family, are found throughout the tropics with a small number occurring in temperate regions. They have a very distinctive inflorescence, consisting of a fleshy spike bearing numerous small flowers called the spadix, partly surrounded by a large, often coloured, bract, called the spathe.

Although all aroids produce this characteristic inflorescence, in other ways they are very different. There is even a free-floating aquatic member known as water-lettuce (*Pista stratiotes*) which grows in stagnant water. Its small white spathe arises from a rosette of spongy-textured leaves.

Many of the tropical species have been introduced into cultivation. The Swiss cheese plant (*Monstera deliciosa*), a native of Mexico, is a climber with large leaves perforated by slits and holes. Dieffenbachias are also grown for their foliage. Anthuriums and zantedeschias are both cultivated for their colourful inflorescences. The latter are popularly known as arum lilies and they originate from South Africa where several different species occur. The one most commonly found in cultivation is *Zantedeschia aethiopica* which has become so successfully established in parts of Australia that it is now considered to be a weed.

Also found in cultivation is the mouse-tail plant (*Arisarum proboscideum*) from southern Europe which has a long, thin extension to its purplish spathe resembling the tail of a mouse. *Sauromatium venosum*, popularly known as the voodoo lily, is sometimes sold as a curiosity for growing on a window-sill because leaves and an inflorescence will grow from its corm without the need for soil.

Many aroids emit strong smells which are unpleasant to us but very attractive to insects. The western skunk cabbage (*Lysichiton americanum*) is aptly named but the small flying beetles which pollinate the flowers seem to like it. The giant *Amorphophallus titanum* from Sumatra has a massive inflorescence nearly two metres tall which produces a stench likened to the smell of rotting fish and is also pollinated by beetles. It has a single large leaf which grows from an enormous underground tuber, about 60cm.

Small flies are attracted to the cuckoo-pint (*Arum maculatum*) by its smell. Its flowers are situated at the base of the spadix with the females in a ring at the bottom and the males arranged on top. Above is a layer of downward-pointing hairs. The partly surrounding spathe has an oily surface inside and visiting flies become trapped, unable to climb back up again because of the slippery surface and the stiff hairs. The female flowers are mature and will be pollinated if the insects are carrying pollen from another arum of the same species. The next day the male flowers mature and their pollen dusts the flies as they make their escape, the hairs having shrivelled and the walls dried out in the meantime.

Bananas and Birds of Paradise

Banana plants look like trees but in fact they are the world's largest herbs. The 'trunks' have no woody support tissue but are soft, pulpy columns formed by the closely sheathed bases of the leaves. The real stems of the banana grow underground, branching freely and sending up the leafy pseudostems from basal corms. The remarkable inflorescence grows up through the pseudostem, emerging at the top where it hangs downwards like a pendulum.

A series of large coloured bracts initially protect the clusters of flowers, falling away as the familiar bunches or hands of bananas develop. The female flowers, which give rise to the fruits, are found on the lower part of the inflorescence while the male flowers grow towards the top.

The fruits of wild bananas are inedible, containing numerous seeds but very little flesh. The numerous cultivated forms, which have arisen by hydridisation, contain no seeds only the characteristic pulpy, white flesh. Fruits for export are cut while still green and allowed to ripen on the voyage. They are not fully ripe until the skin is speckled with brown marks. Because they set no seed, cultivated bananas are all clones, new plants being grown from suckers.

Left **A conveyor is being used to transport freshly cut green bananas on this plantation.**

Right **Bright colours, especially yellow, are very attractive to birds. Strelitzias use this fact to advertise their flowers.**

Below **The bird of paradise flower does indeed look like the crested head of an exotic bird.**

Bananas are jungle plants originating in South-east Asia. With the aid of man they have spread throughout the tropics where they are now a staple food. Dessert bananas come mainly from *Musa acuminata*. The fruits of a second species, *M. x paradisiaca*, are known as plantains or cooking bananas which are eaten fried or boiled. Other species produce the fibre known as manilla hemp and the leaves are used for thatching. The flowering banana, *M. coccinea*, is grown for its ornamental scarlet bracts. Some of the wild species are quite bizarre — one even produces self-peeling fruits!

Right **Five different varieties of banana. The Gros Michel is the commonest dessert banana while the plantain is used in cooking. The other three are less well-known varieties.**

Below **Musa textilis is the source of manilla hemp, made from the coarse fibres of the leaf stalks.**

Below, right **A banana inflorescence droops downwards so that the top is nearest the ground. The flowers towards the base of the inflorescence are female, those at the tip are male. The red bracts protect the young flowers.**

Strelitzias are close relatives of bananas. Some are quite large and tree-like but the best known species, the bird of paradise flower, *Strelitzia reginae*, only reaches a height of a little over one metre. However its similarity to bananas shows in the leaves, which are large and oblong. In its native South Africa it can be found on river banks and in clearings along the coast of Cape Province.

Like the banana, the bird of paradise flower has become widely cultivated, but for its striking flowers not its fruits. Each 'flower' is really a complete inflorescence enclosed in a horizontal sheath. The flowers have orange sepals and blue petals and emerge one by one at roughly weekly intervals. These complex flowers are adapted to pollination by sunbirds and sugarbirds. Two of the blue petals form a tube enclosing the anthers and style. When a bird perches on the horizontal sheath and attempts to feed its weight causes the tip of the style to brush against its breast. Pressure on the petal tube showers pollen from the anthers onto the bird to be picked up by the style of the next flowers visited. In turn this action releases a third petal blocking the nectaries, allowing the bird to sip the nectar.

Apple Banana

Lady Finger

Gros Michel

Red Banana

Plantain

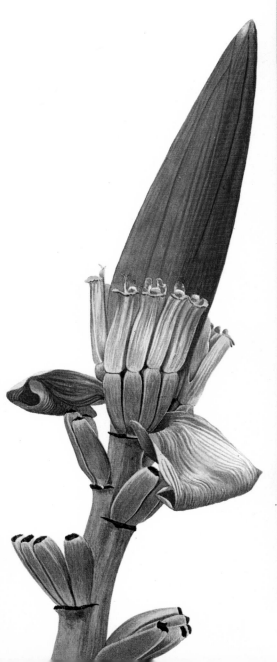

Deciduous Forests

A deciduous forest in winter presents a stark scene. The trees are bare and the ground apparently lifeless, but the deciduous nature of the trees is the factor which allows such forests one of their great glories — the beautiful carpet of flowers which covers the ground in spring.

During the summer months the trees screen out the sun, producing light intensities too low for most ground level plants to survive. In autumn and winter light levels increase as the canopy thins but temperatures are too low for growth. With the return of warm weather in spring there is a short period when light conditions on the forest floor are suitable for herbaceous plants — if they can grow fast enough to take advantage. These plants flower in early spring before the trees begin to leaf up and they are shaded out once more.

The early spring forest flowers are generally perennials, often bulbs, which can get away to a flying start as soon as conditions are suitable for growth. Species such as bluebells, primroses and anemones are common and often form large colonies, covering the ground with blossom.

The early spring flora is followed by plants which are shade-tolerant and flower when the trees are already in leaf. Plants such as wood sorrel and dog's mercury are very tolerant of shade and may even become dominant in beech woods.

Among the more unusual forest denizens are the saprophytes such as bird's nest and ghost orchids. Saprophytes do not photosynthesise. Instead they form a partnership with a mycorrhizal fungus which allows them to feed on decaying matter. Having no need of sunlight these plants can grow in deepest shade. They lack green pigmentation and their pale flower-spikes show up clearly in the gloom of the deep forest.

The herbaceous flora varies between different forest types, partly as a result of variation in the canopy produced by the different trees. Oak and ash for example have a relatively light canopy and tend to leaf up fairly late in spring. This allows quite a range of plants to grow beneath the trees. Beech produces a denser canopy and greater shade. The leaves are quite thick and set in a close pattern on the twigs, allowing little light through. Beech leaves are very slow to rot down and the layer of leaf litter on the forest floor can be quite deep. This also helps to keep down the number of plants growing there.

Most of the world's deciduous forests grow in the most highly populated regions of the Northern Hemisphere, in Europe, eastern North America and China. Inevitably these forests have been affected by man's activities, particularly in Europe where there is virtually no virgin forest remaining. Much of the forests has been cut down, sometimes being replaced with evergreen coniferous species. This has greatly reduced the old deciduous forest flora but not all of man's activities have had adverse effects — at least on the herbaceous plants. The old practise of coppicing, in which trees are regularly cut to ground level to produce new growth encourages flowers — at least temporarily — by opening up the habitat to extra light and air. Similarly, natural glades and clearings, for example where trees have fallen, woodland rides and the forest margins are reasonably open habitats occupied by a range of grasses and flowers.

Above **Surely one of the loveliest sights of spring is a carpet of bluebells on a woodland floor. Bluebells are slow to colonise new woodland so the best displays are found in very old woods.**

Opposite, top left **The saprophytic bird's nest orchid (*Neottia nidis avis*) grows in beech woods.**

Opposite bottom **The ground flora of a coppiced wood is richest in newly cut areas. As the trees re-grow the ground flora gradually diminishes until it is shaded out completely. When the trees are cut again the ground flora rapidly re-establishes itself and the cycle continues.**

Below **Plants which find the light intensity under the tree canopy too low may colonise open areas such as woodland rides.**

Below, right **Shade tolerant plants which grow in deciduous forests and woods include** (*from left to right*) **dogs mercury and wood sorrel.** (*Opposite, middle left*) **Ransoms.**

In the summer the canopy of a deciduous forest screens out the sun.

newly cut area

3-years' growth

grasses and brambles between stools

stools

standard trees

drainage ditch

ride

7-years' growth

most of ground flora shaded-out

rich ground flora between stools – violets, Primroses, Bluebells, Bugle, Dog's Mercury, etc.

Orchids

Orchids belong to one of the largest families of flowering plants and they come in all shapes and sizes, showing an astonishing variety. Nobody quite knows how many different species there are, but there are probably well over eighteen thousand. Their distribution is worldwide with nearly every country having one or more representatives, occurring in practically every type of habitat, from tropical forests to deserts, and from mountains to lowland marshes.

Many of the orchids in the tropics are epiphytes, growing on the branches of trees. Some even grow upside down with their roots sticking up into the air and the stems hanging downwards. However, most of the species found in temperate areas live on the ground. Some are saprophytes, living off dead and decaying humus. One Australian species has been discovered that lives its life completely underground, flowers and all.

The orchid flower is quite unlike any other and is considered to be one of the most highly advanced in the plant kingdom, being specialized for attracting insect pollinators. They vary in size from a few millimetres across to 30cm or more. At one stage during the development of the flower it twists through 180°, so in fact all the orchid flowers you see are really upside down.

The reproductive organs are borne on a compound structure with a solitary stamen at the top. The pollen is all massed together into clumps called pollinia. Each pollinium consists of thousands of individual grains; an insect visiting the orchid is likely to leave with this mass stuck to its head.

Each type of orchid is usually adapted to attract one particular type of insect and in some cases these adaptations are quite remarkable. The flowers of the mirror orchid (*Ophrys speculum*), a Mediterranean species, appear when the bees that pollinate them are searching for a mate. The flowers bear such a striking resemblance to the female bee that males are fooled into trying to copulate with the flowers, pollinating them as they do so.

Many orchids are cultivated for their beautiful, and often fragrant flowers. Plant collectors went to great lengths to bring back new and exotic species from tropical countries, but unfortunately many of these died because they were not given the conditions they needed. It is now known that orchid seeds will not germinate successfully unless they become infected with a mycorrhizal fungus. The tiny seedlings live saprophytically for the first part of their life and obtain nutrients from the fungus because the seeds are so tiny that they contain no food reserves of their own. As soon as the plants become successfully established they lose their dependence on the fungus and manufacture their own food.

The only species of orchid cultivated not for its flowers, but for its fruit, is the vanilla orchid from Mexico (*Vanilla planifolia*) whose pods are used to provide the flavouring for vanilla essence.

Left The flowers of this species of *Ophrys* resemble a type of female bee. Note the sticky mass of pollen in the bottom flower which will adhere to the male bee when it attempts to make with the flower.

Opposite, right The vanilla orchid (*Vanilla planifolia*).

Opposite, right Orchid flowers are quite unlike any other. These weird blooms belong to a ground-dwelling species, *Corybas oblongus*.

Above **Odontoglossum** 'Amabile', a hybrid produced artificially in cultivation.

Below Not all orchids have large showy flowers. The common twayblade has such small, insignificant flowers that it is easily overlooked.

Lilies

One of the largest flowering plant families is the Lily family. It has a cosmopolitan distribution, lilies and their allies being found in all parts of the world. A few species are large, evergreen succulents, such as the aloes, or climbers, such as the glory lily (*Gloriosa*), but the vast majority are perennial herbs which grow from bulbs, corms or rhizomes.

As a family the lilies are very variable in the shape of their leaves and the size and colour of their flowers. However the arrangement of the floral parts — perianth segments, stamens and styles — is fairly constant, in whorls of three or multiples of three. The two whorls of perianth segments are usually separate, the three inner segments sometimes larger and more colourful than the other three, but all six may be fused to form a tubular flower as in red-hot poker (*Kniphofia*).

Probably the most beautiful flowers in the whole family belong to species of *Lilium*, the true lilies. They are large and showy, with prominent stamens and are borne in sprays with the flowers erect, horizontal or pendulous relative to the stem. There is a rich variety of colours and shapes, some like flaring trumpets, others bowl or star-shaped. In the turk's-cap lily (*L. martagon*) the perianth segments are curled back to resemble the shape of a turban. Not surprisingly they have long attracted gardeners and have been cultivated for centuries.

Many other genera are attractive and of great horitcultural importance, such as *Muscari* (grape hyacinth), *Agapanthus* (African lily), *Hemerocallis* (day lily), *Colchicum* (autumn crocus), *Kniphofia* (red-hot poker), *Hosta* (plantain lily) and *Convallaria* (lily-of-the-valley). That well known and widely grown vegetable the onion and its relatives belong to the genus *Allium*. This and *Asparagus* are the only genera of any agricultural importance in the family.

Left, above **Fritillaria meleagris is the snake's-head or leopard lily.**

Opposite, top left **Lily-of-the-valley is one of the fragrant lilies.**

Below **Lilies have been prized since antiquity for the beauty of their flowers.**

Right **Horticulturalists have bred tulips to produce a range of colours.**

Bulbs and Corms

A bulb is an underground storage organ consisting of swollen and fleshy leaves, or sometimes leaf bases, tightly packed together. The leaves may be narrow and all separate from each other as in the lilies or very broad and wrapped around each other and enclosed in a brown, papery covering — an arrangement referred to as tunicated and found, for example, in onions. At the base of the bulb is a 'plate' from which the roots grow. This plate represents the very much shortened and flattened stem. The centre of a dormant bulb contains the next season's shoot with a complete, though undeveloped, set of leaves and flowers.

Bulbs often produce offsets or bulblets, small bulbs which form at the side of the main bulb, eventually separating to grow new plants. Bulblets should not be confused with the similar bulbils, which are produced above ground in the flower-heads. They are typical of many *Allium* species in which the flowers may be completely replaced by bulbils.

A corm is similar to a bulb in being an underground storage organ. It differs in being formed from a swollen stem base and is a single, solid mass of starchy tissue. The bud is on the top of the corm and each year a new corm is formed on top of the old one.

Right **Bulbs and corms are often confused with each other. Although they perform similar functions as storage organs, they are structurally quite different.**

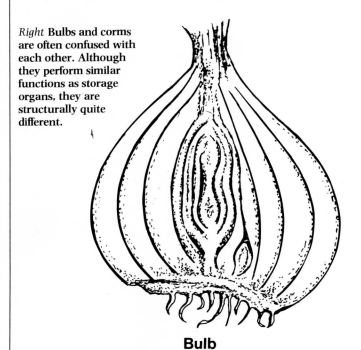

Bulb

Corm

Grasslands

The most impressive pastures in the world are the great open grasslands, the North American prairie, South American pampa, Asian steppe and African savanna or veldt. These vast areas are natural grasslands, partly maintained by a relatively low rainfall which discourages the growth of woody plants. Grasslands receiving high rainfall, such as those in much of Europe and Australasia, were formerly forested and would revert to this state if tree and shrub seedlings were not deliberately removed.

The other major factor which helps to maintain grasslands, both natural and artificial, is grazing. All the great grasslands support large herds of grazing animals which soon eat off and destroy plants not adapted to meet such demands. Grasses survive because their unique structure allows them to grow despite periodic grazing.

Most plants have their growing points — the meristems — situated at the tips of the shoots which grow longer from the top. If the tips are eaten, and the meristems destroyed, the plant is prevented from growing and repeated grazing soon kills it. The meristems of a grass are situated at the base of the stem and just above each joint in the stem, which lengthens from the bottom up. Similarly, each leaf has a meristem situated at the point where the blade and sheath join, so repeated loss of the upper parts of the stem and leaves does not prevent further growth. In addition grasses grow very quickly, soon recovering from the effects of grazing or mowing.

Grasses are slender, even fragile-looking plants but they are deceptively tough and compete successfully with other species. They often form dense tufts or tussocks with extensive root-systems. Many spread by

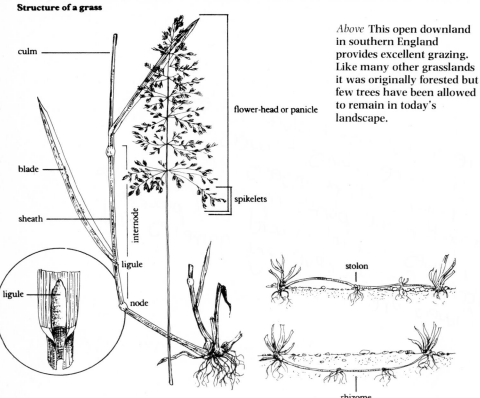

Structure of a grass

culm

blade

sheath

ligule

ligule

node

internode

flower-head or panicle

spikelets

stolon

rhizome

Above This open downland in southern England provides excellent grazing. Like many other grasslands it was originally forested but few trees have been allowed to remain in today's landscape.

Opposite, top right
Water meadows provide homes for many flowers. They are often used for hay and are left ungrazed between March and July, allowing the plants time to flower and seed.

Opposite, bottom right
Rosette plants hug the ground to avoid being eaten. However some, such as cowslip (*Primula veris*) send up taller flower spikes to advertise their flowers to pollinating insects.

Right **Some plants have evolved protective devices to discourage grazing animals. These spiny thistles grow unmolested by the sheep, in contrast to the rest of the pasture which has been heavily grazed.**

Right **Fires are a natural hazard in grasslands during the dry season. Once started, a fire can rapidly sweep across huge areas since there are few barriers to its progress. Savannah fires like this may be spectacular, but do not kill all of the plants, many of which have developed remarkable powers of regeneration.**

means of creeping rhizomes or stolons, forming the characterisic sward or turf associated only with grasses.

Open grasslands are often windswept and grasses utilise this aspect of their environment by being wind-pollinated. Like all such plants grasses produce copious amounts of pollen which can be carried for miles — to the misery of hay-fever sufferers.

Of course grasses are not the only plants to be found in pastures. In fact grasslands have a surprisingly wide array of flowers which can produce rich displays of colour against the green background. Finding room to grow in the densely packed sward is not easy and many of the flowers are perennials which do not need to re-establish themselves each year.

Like the grasses, these plants must survive grazing and mowing. Some species are unpalatable or poisonous to animals, or are armed with thorns or spines, and are left unmolested while surrounding plants are grazed. Species not protected in this way may have rosettes of leaves or creeping leafy shoots which are low enough to avoid damage, only the flowering stems growing to any appreciable height. Others have annually renewable stems and most produce buds at, or just below, soil-level where protection is greatest. In this way growth can be resumed even if the higher aerial parts are damaged.

Cereals

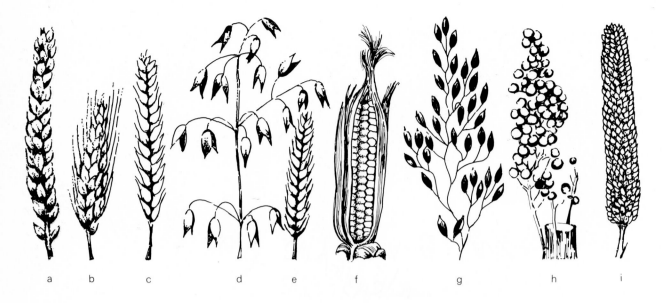

Left The ears of some of the principal cereals.
a. bread wheat,
b. durum wheat, c. rye,
d. oats, e. barley,
f. maize, g. rice,
h. sorghum, i. millet.

Below, left Cereals differ from other grasses in not easily releasing the ripe grains from the ears. This allows the crop to be harvested with little loss of grain.

Right Rice paddies are deliberately flooded to provide the right conditions for the young plants.

Undoubtedly the most important group of plants in the world from mankind's point of view are the cereals. Everywhere they provide staple foods and are the most widely grown crops. Cereals have been grown for many thousands of years, probably since man first began farming on a primitive scale. All have evolved from wild grasses but very gradually varieties have been selected which show desirable characters such as larger grains, easier separation of grain from chaff and so on. This improvement has increased rapidly in modern times with the deliberate use of breeding techniques to produce varieties with greater yields and increased resistance to disease.

Cereals are ideal crop plants. They can be sown densely to give a high yield from a small area. They are easy to sow and harvest, particularly with machinery and the dry grain has excellent storage properties. Most important of all, cereals are highly nutritious, probably more so than any other plants. Wheat for example yields sugars, fats, proteins and vitamins as well as starch!

On a world scale there are seven major cereals, as well as a number of minor ones.

Wheat The principal cereal and the most widely grown. High-yield areas include much of North America, Europe, Asia and Australia.

Rice The most productive of all the grain crops. The young plants require marshy conditions so they are grown in specially flooded areas known as paddy fields. Rice is the staple food of much of India, China and South-east Asia.

Maize The most widely distributed of the cereals and grown in most parts of the world, though often on a small scale. A very ancient crop with obscure origins.

Sorghum or Guinea corn Sorghum, along with millet, is a principal crop in the drier tropics where it withstands drought and poor soils well. The major growing region is Africa.

Rye, oats and barley Three more cereals which flourish on poor soils, mainly in temperate and even sub-arctic regions and grown in much of Europe and North Africa.

An important non-cereal crop from the tropics is sugar cane. Most grasses have a hollow main stem, but that of sugar cane is filled with a tough pith from which the sugar is extracted.

Among the most successful and useful species are the bamboos, giant woody grasses which can reach heights of 30m or more. The decorative wood is light but strong and has many uses, in furniture, buildings and even clothes.

As well as cereals and other crops the importance of grasses as indirect foods should not be overlooked. Much of the meat we eat comes from animals raised entirely on the rich grazing provided by these plants.

Above **Modern methods of cereal production rely heavily on the use of machinery.**

Above **Some cereals, e.g. wheat and barley, can be sown in autumn to produce an early crop in the following summer.**

Left **Driving animals over corn to thresh the grain is an ancient method still in use in poorer parts of the world.**

Origin of Bread Wheat

Wild Einkorn (wild wheat)

Aegilops Speltoides (wild grass)

hybridisation

Wild Emmer (wild wheat)

Durum Wheat (cultivated wheat)

Emmer (cultivated wheat)

Aegilops Squarrosa (wild grass)

Both hybridisations were natural, not artificial

hybridisation

Spelt Wheat (cultivated)

Bread wheat (cultivated)

Above **The origin of wheat: modern wheats are believed to have arisen via several hybridisation events, some accidental, some quite deliberate, the whole process occurring over many centuries.**

47

Mediterranean Regions

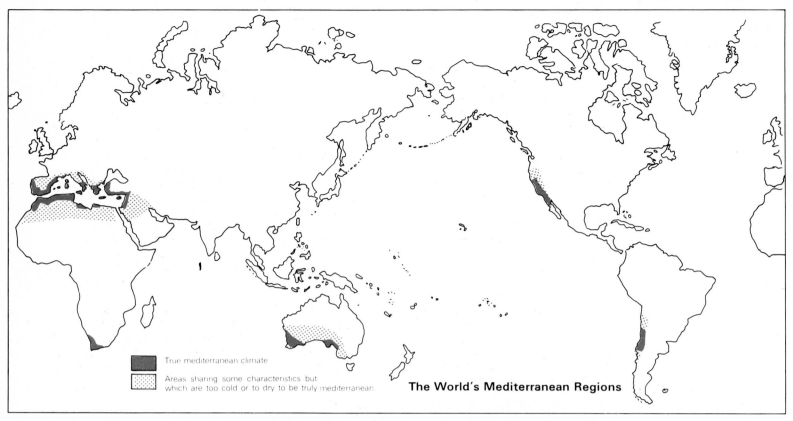

True mediterranean climate

Areas sharing some characteristics but which are too cold or to dry to be truly mediterranean

The World's Mediterranean Regions

Mediterranean regions can be found on six of the world's seven continents. The most extensive regions occur around the Mediterranean Sea which has lent its name to this type of climate; similar areas occur in California, the Cape Province of South Africa, Western and Southern Australia and western South America. Despite its wide distribution this type of habitat is rare, occurring only where specific climatic and geographical conditions coincide and covers only about one per cent of the earth's surface. It is, however, a clearly defined and easily recognisable habitat characterised by a particular type of vegetation.

For a region to be classed as Mediterranean it must have a climate which falls within very precise limits. Although well known for their warm and equitable climate, Mediterranean areas do have a definite winter, though mild and without frequent or severe frosts. The rainfall is sufficient for abundant vegetation, but too little to support large trees other than those adapted to dry conditions. Most of the rain falls in winter; the summer months are arid.

The most characteristic vegetation is known as maquis or garigue in Europe, fynbos in South Africa and, particularly in America, by the most widely applied name, chapparal. Chapparal communities are dominated by sclerophyllous plants — evergreen shrubs and low trees with small, dark leathery leaves. They are drought resistant, able to survive the arid conditions and to take advantage of the two short growing seasons, in spring and early winter. Many species produce aromatic resins and oils in the leaves which are given off in the heat of the day.

Forests are rare but do occur in Mediterranean lands. Trees are restricted by the limited rainfall and — increasingly — by man's activities, and it is more usual to find isolated individuals or small stands and thickets. Like the shrubs, most are sclerophyllous species. Eucalyptus and conifers such as Stone pine are common. The latter may seem surprising at first, conifers normally being associated with cold lands. However they are very drought resistant and the Stone pine withstands the hot, dry summers better than most.

Summer is the adverse season for herbaceous plants too. Many avoid it by flowering early then resting till winter as rootstocks or bulbs.

Summer is also the season of fires, to which chapparal is very prone. They can cause erosion if followed by storms.

Fires play an important role here. Most plants have already dried out and died back by summer. Fire reduces the remains to ash, releasing tied up minerals. It burns litter and also affects the upper soil, destroying a 'non-wettable' layer which builds up near the surface and prevents water getting through to the roots beneath. Most plants survive, often sprouting again within ten days of the fire. The same shrubs will eventually dominate the vegetation again. In California 'fire-type' annuals — normally rare — take advantage of the newly cleared ground and can be very common for a few years, gradually disappearing as the shrubs regain their former prominence.

The equilibrium between chapparal vegetation and climatic conditions is fragile. The vegetation does not re-establish easily and transformation into arable land is usually irreversible. The plants have an important protective role and, once removed, erosion rapidly sets in.

Older-style cultivation methods such as terracing partially restrict such effects but modern methods are less successful in preventing serious damage to the landscape.

All of the world's Mediterranean regions except South Africa and Australia occur in geologically young and unstable areas. The Mediterranean climate itself only originated during the recent Pleistocene era. When the polar ice-caps melt, summer rainfall will return to the lands and the Mediterranean regions, with their distinctive vegetation, will disappear.

Above **Terracing steep slopes to enable them to be farmed more easily is a common agricultural technique in the Mediterranean hills.**

Above, right **European maquis is typically dominated by low evergreen shrubs such as brooms, lavenders and rosemary.**

Right **Legumes such as *Hedysarum coronarium* are major constituents of Mediterranean vegetation.**

Opposite, bottom **Conifers are quite common around the Mediterranean. These umbrella-shaped stone pines, *Pinus pinea*, are indicative of light sandy soils.**

Proteas and Banksias

The Proteaceae includes some 1000 species occurring throughout the Southern Hemisphere and extending just north of the equator in Central America, Africa and Asia. But they show their greatest diversity in the Mediterranean regions of South Africa and Australia where they often form the dominant broad-leaved elements of fynbos and malee vegetation. In South Africa the main genera are *Protea*, *Leucospermum* and *Leucadendron*. The equivalent genera in Australia are *Banksia*, named after the famous English botanist Sir Joseph Banks, and *Hakea*.

Most Proteaceae are shrubby while some form trees of considerable size. All have large, showy and frequently spectacular inflorescences to attract the insects and birds such as the cape sugarbird which act as pollinators. The inflorescences are generally cone-shaped and contain up to 1000 flowers.

These often have very prominent, curved styles, and brightly coloured or bearded bracts enhance the overall effect. After pollination the dry, shrivelled flowers remain attached giving a distinctive, shaggy look to the cone.

The Proteaceae are superbly adapted for surviving the seasonal hazard of bush-fires. Indeed a number of species actually depend on fires to maintain them in a vigorous, free-flowering state. Plants which have not suffered recent burning become straggly and senescent.

Many of the trees and larger shrubs have very thick, fibrous bark which protects them from the flames. They can even survive severe damage to their crowns in this way, new growth developing from under the bark layers of the stems and main branches. The smaller shrubs and the seedlings of tree species produce lignotubers — tough, well-

Protea eximia (*top right*) and *P. cynaroides* (*above*) are found in South Africa. *P. cynaroides*, the giant protea, is the national flower of South Africa.

B. burdettii (*bottom right*) is found in Western Australia, *B. burdettii* in shady heathlands, *B. baxteri* (*right, middle*) in more marshy areas.

Above **After experiencing the heat of a bush fire these banksia capsules have opened to release their seeds.**

protected rootstocks beneath the surface of the soil. After the fire has passed, destroying the above ground growth in the process, the lignotubers send up new aerial shoots.

Not all Proteaceae can survive the effects of fire. Some species are killed outright and these must survive in the form of seeds which can sprout after the fire has passed. Here again the importance of periodic burning is seen, fires providing the seeds with an excellent environment in which to germinate. The minerals and trace elements contained in old growth are reduced to ash, enriching the soil. The ground is cleared of scrub, allowing light to reach the seedlings, and plants which compete for water and nutrients are swept away, giving the new generation of plants a chance to establish themselves.

Fire appears to have played a major role in the evolution of the Australian banksias. *Proteaceae* in general retain the dry fruiting cones for some months before releasing their seeds. Banksias have taken this one step further, the application of heat being required before the hard capsules will open to release their winged seeds. The dried capsules may remain on the plant for many years before a bush fire induces the opening response.

Top **Buds, fully open flowers and an old fruiting head are here all found together on the same plant of *Banksia menziesii*.**

Above **These immature flower heads show the typical 'cone-like' structure found in many banksias.**

Gourds

Some of the world's most variable and attractive fruits are to be found among the gourds and their allies. Such fruits are a kind of berry, technically known as a 'pepo', that is a large, single-celled fruit with pulpy flesh surrounding numerous seeds. All members of the family to which gourds belong, the Cucurbitaceae, have this type of fruit, but within the single type they show a bewildering variety of shapes, sizes and colours. They also rank among the heaviest fruits in the world!

The Cucurbitaceae include some of the most ancient and important crop plants,

particularly in those parts of the world where subsistence farming is widespread. In fact, though many wild species are cultivated, a number have arisen in cultivation and have no wild counterparts.

Gourds are widely grown in subtropical and Mediterranean regions. They need a great deal of sunshine and are, in fact, well adapted to semi-arid conditions. Their massive root systems and very rapid growth allow them to mature and ripen their fruits in a short growing season. Gourds are also grown in the tropics but with rather less success. Here the fruits are more prone to

disease and rot in the humid conditions.

All gourds are herbaceous vines and either trail along the ground or climb by means of clasping tendrils. They have hairy, lobed leaves and large, unisexual white or yellow flowers. The edible species are all annuals. The name gourd is actually applied to fruits which have a hard, durable rind. Most are edible when young but they are usually grown for ornament or to provide containers. The yellow-flowered gourds of North America are all variants of *Cucurbita pepo* var. *ovifera*. White-flowered gourds belong to a number of different genera and

How gourds climb

Climbing gourds do so by means of clasping tendrils. A single sometimes branched tendril grows from the axil of each leaf. The tendril becomes sensitive to touch when about one-third grown, this sensitivity increasing as growth continues. On making firm contact with any kind of support the tendril begins to wrap around it. Reaction time between contact and the start of coiling varies from two minutes to as little as twenty seconds. At this stage, woody tissue may be laid down to provide extra strength. As well as coiling around the support, the tendril coils along its own length like a spring. This allows the tendril to provide firm but flexible support with enough 'give' to prevent it being snapped by sudden movement such as the wind.

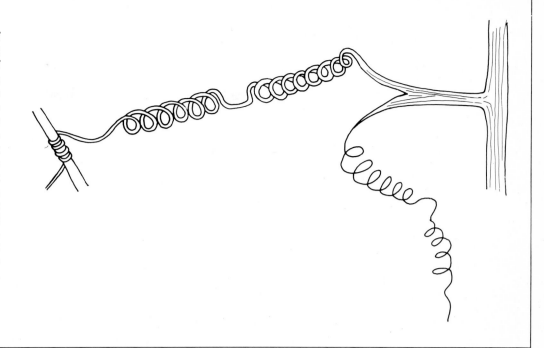

include bottle-gourds, ivy-gourds and luffas. These are mainly Old World species.

Soft-rind fruits include melons, pumpkins and winter squash. Melons are the fruits of *Cucumis melo*. They have sweet, fragrant flesh and are popular as desserts. Water melons belong to another genus, *Citrullus*.

Opposite **All members of the gourd family produce separate male and female flowers, the male flowers usually opening a few days before the female flowers. Both sexes are large, funnel-shaped and usually white or bright yellow in colour. The striking flowers are followed by no less spectacular fruits which occur in a bewildering array of shapes, sizes and colours, just a few of which are shown here.**

There are numerous kinds of marrow, squash and pumpkin, but most are derived from just four species of *Cucurbita*: *C.pepo*, *C.mixta*, *C.maxima* and *C.moschata*. Squashes are divided into two types, winter and summer squash. Summer squashes are derived from *C.pepo* and include courgettes

and zuchini. They are eaten before they are ripe, after which they become too fibrous to be palatable. Winter squashes are derived from all four species. They have darker flesh than the summer varieties and are picked when ripe for storage through winter. They are less fibrous and more nutritious than the summer squashes.

Below **Squirting cucumber (*Ecbalium elaterium*) has explosive fruits. When ripe just a touch is enough to separate fruit from stalk. The pressure of fluid inside the fruit then forcibly squirts the seeds out in a jet-like stream.**

Deserts

The horse latitudes which girdle the earth between 30°N and 35°S are the regions of the world's great deserts. Deserts receive little or no rainfall for much of the year and the air is hot and dry. Winds blow constantly during the day, carrying abrasive sand and dust.

Rainfall is erratic but when it does come it is often heavy, causing flash floods and gouging out channels in soils unprotected by trees and grass. Some of the water is lost immediately as run-off and more evaporates under the drying sun and wind. Little penetrates far into the soil.

Heat and drought are only two of the problems facing desert plants. The clear skies which let deserts heat up quickly during the day also allow the reverse effect and desert nights are cold, so the plants must withstand a wide range of temperatures. The light is intense with high levels of harmful ultra-violet radiation. Overall a hostile environment; in spite of this, a remarkably varied plant life thrives in all but the most arid regions.

The greatest threat to survival for desert plants is undoubtedly drought and they must be efficient in their collection and use of water. They have large, spreading root systems to catch as much of the meagre rainfall as possible. Most are shallow, since water does not penetrate deep into the soil, but the roots of trees such as mesquite reach deep into the ground – up to about 24m – to find more permanent sources of water. Any aid to collection may be used. The shape and arrangement of the leaves of yuccas and aloes for example helps to channel water towards the roots.

Many desert plants store water, frequently in succulent stems and leaves. Such organs are fleshy and swollen with water-storing tissue. Roots and tubers may also act as reservoirs.

Having obtained water, the plants must be frugal with it and there are many adaptations geared towards minimising water-loss. Structures with large surface areas lose water quickly by evaporation and large, thin leaves are a luxury desert plants cannot afford. They tend to have small and sometimes extremely reduced leaves which are often waxy or leathery.

A few plants use more direct strategies. The hardy creosote bush secretes poisons which kill neighbouring plants, reducing the competition for water.

Such adaptations are not found in the numerous desert annuals, which simply avoid the unfavourable periods, surviving as seeds until suitable conditions occur, immediately after the rains. Then the entire desert blossoms into brief but colourful life. The seeds must germinate, grow, flower and set new seed before drought returns and the plants die. The whole sequence may be over in a few short weeks.

Opposite, top left **Clear blue skies, an eroded landscape dotted with small, hardy plants— a typical scene for much of the desert year.**

Opposite, top right **Soap-tree yucca (*Yucca elata*) growing in dunes in White Sands National Monument, New Mexico, U.S.A.**

Opposite, middle **Flash floods in the desert gouge out erosion gullies.**

Opposite, bottom **Creosote bushes scattered over the desert sand. This tough customer is one of nature's winners, poisoning any competitors for the scarce resources of the desert.**

Right **Leaf adaptations to water loss. *Lithops leslieii* has very succulent leaves. Compass plant can orientate its leaves away from the sun's rays.**
***Fenestraria rhopalophylla* has succulent leaves with special windows which control the light entering them.**
Marram grass rolls up its leaves to protect the stomata.

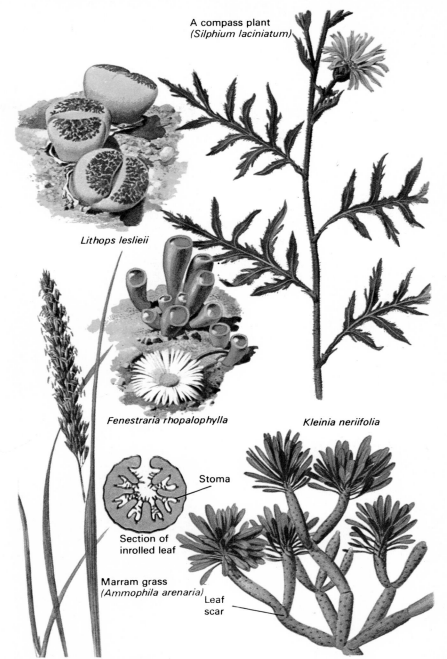

A compass plant
(*Silphium laciniatum*)

Lithops leslieii

Fenestraria rhopalophylla

Kleinia neriifolia

Stoma

Section of inrolled leaf

Marram grass
(*Ammophila arenaria*)

Leaf scar

Below, left **Brachystelma barberiae** relies on its massive tuber in order to survive adverse conditions.

Below Sturt's desert pea has hairy leaves which cut down water loss and brilliantly coloured flowers.

Cacti

Cacti are regarded as classic plants of the arid 'bad lands' of North America, though they do, in fact, grow in a range of habitats including tropical rain forest. All desert plants have some adaptations to a water-scarce environment but cacti have refined these adaptations to a remarkable degree.

Cacti are well known for their ability to store water. This is done by the stems and is best shown in the barrel-cacti where the cylinder-shaped stems are swollen with water-storing tissue. Such is the capacity of the stems that they can survive for years without replenishing their stores. The stems are often pleated to form 'ribs' running lengthwise down the stem. These ribs allow the stems to expand as they take up water and to contract again as the reserves are depleted. The shape which has the lowest surface area in relation to its volume is a sphere. A few cacti approach this overall shape to minimise evaporation losses. Odd though it seems, they grow in the shade of their own bodies.

Some primitive cacti are leafy but in the desert leaves can be a serious source of water loss and in most cacti they have been highly modified or even dispensed with altogether. Their photosynthetic function is taken over by the stem which has become green for this purpose.

Although the leaves no longer function in the normal way they do not disappear completely. Some have been modified and reduced to form the spines which give cacti their formidable reputation (though there are spineless species). The spines sit on organs called areoles or spine cushions, developed from modified side shoots. The pattern formed by the areoles can be a clue to the identity of different species.

Right **The plants in this specially designed garden show the variety of size and form in cacti.**

Below **Two species of *Pseudolobivia*. Note the ribs which allow the succulent stems to expand.**

One obvious function of spines is protection, for in the sparse desert vegetation any plant is under threat of being eaten. But spines also play an important role in temperature regulation by providing shade for the plant. For example the old man cactus (*Cephalocereus senilis*) is covered with woolly, white, hair-like spines which reflect light and help insulate the stem. *Mammilaria theresae* has spines shaped like miniature parasols which keep off the sun. Spines are even involved in water collection. Droplets of dew condense on them and are then absorbed through the spines into the cactus body.

Cacti are confined to the New World where they may be dominant plants in the deserts. One of the finest sights are the giant saguero cacti which can reach heights of 12m or so. Their huge candelabra shapes are widely separated from each other because the shallow, spreading root systems must collect as much water as possible and so

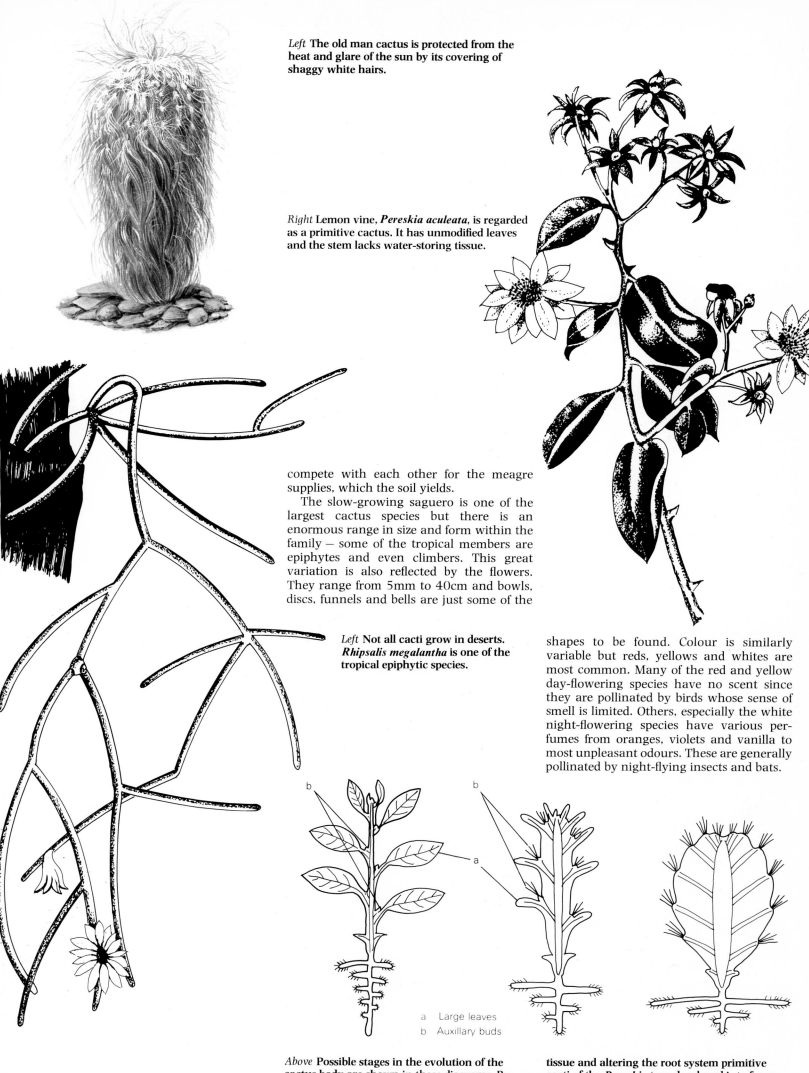

Left **The old man cactus is protected from the heat and glare of the sun by its covering of shaggy white hairs.**

Right **Lemon vine, *Pereskia aculeata*, is regarded as a primitive cactus. It has unmodified leaves and the stem lacks water-storing tissue.**

compete with each other for the meagre supplies, which the soil yields.

The slow-growing saguero is one of the largest cactus species but there is an enormous range in size and form within the family — some of the tropical members are epiphytes and even climbers. This great variation is also reflected by the flowers. They range from 5mm to 40cm and bowls, discs, funnels and bells are just some of the

Left **Not all cacti grow in deserts. *Rhipsalis megalantha* is one of the tropical epiphytic species.**

shapes to be found. Colour is similarly variable but reds, yellows and whites are most common. Many of the red and yellow day-flowering species have no scent since they are pollinated by birds whose sense of smell is limited. Others, especially the white night-flowering species have various perfumes from oranges, violets and vanilla to most unpleasant odours. These are generally pollinated by night-flying insects and bats.

a Large leaves
b Auxillary buds

Above **Possible stages in the evolution of the cactus body are shown in these diagrams. By reducing their leaves, developing water storage** tissue and altering the root system primitive cacti of the *Pereskia* type developed into forms like the barrel cacti.

Euphorbias

Above **These three species of African *Euphorbia* all show a remarkable similarity to the desert cacti.**

Below **The flowers of poinsettia are small and yellowish. It is the brightly coloured bracts surrounding them which makes this such a popular house plant.**

Euphorbia is the largest and most fascinating genus belonging to the Spurge family, Euphorbiaceae. It contains over 2000 different species occurring in a wide range of habitats, from the damp, shady woodland floors of temperate regions to the hot, dry deserts of Africa.

Euphorbias show remarkable diversity in habit and structure to suit their particular environment; some are small herbs, others have become shrubby and yet others are large trees. Despite the amazing differences in their growth form, all euphorbias have a very distinctive and highly specialized inflorescence which easily distinguishes them.

The inflorescence is called a cyathium and consists of a small, cup-shaped involucre formed by leaf-like bracts that contain several, often crescent-shaped, glands which secrete an abundant supply of nectar. Within the involucre are a single female flower, which is very simple and consists only of an ovary on a stalk, surrounded by several male flowers which are also greatly reduced and simplified. Flies are attracted by the nectar and normally effect cross-pollination.

The sun spurge (*Euphorbia helioscopia*) has four cyathia and green-coloured bracts, but the poinsettia (*Euphorbia pulcherrima*), a popular house plant at Christmas time, has bracts coloured bright red. Poinsettia occurs naturally in Mexico but is grown extensively in gardens with a warm climate where it can grow up to 3m tall. The variety grown for use as an indoor house plant is specially dwarfed by applying chemicals so that the stems reach no more than 60cm high.

Another euphorbia grown in gardens is the splendid *E. griffithii* from the Himalayas that grows about 75cm tall and has rich orange-coloured bracts.

All euphorbias contain a milky sap or latex in their stems which in some species can be extremely poisonous. In certain parts of Africa euphorbias were planted by the tribesmen around their villages to form a thick, impenetrable hedge to keep out invaders who dared not chop down the plants for fear of the poisonous latex which leaks out profusely if the plants are damaged and causes blindness. The latex was also used for arrow poison. However, by no means all euphorbias are poisonous and some species are used to provide animal fodder. The possibility has also been investigated of producing hydrocarbons similar to petroleum from the sap of certain succulent Euphorbias.

The euphorbias that grow in the dry areas of Africa often show a remarkable similarity to cacti, possessing succulent often thorny, stems for storing water. The tall, columnar stems of *Euphorbia canariensis* are very cactus-like, but the flowers serve to distinguish them as does the location, for cacti naturally grow in the New World whilst euphorbias grow in the Old World.

This striking similarity in structure between two different groups of plants is a classic example of parallel evolution—whereby the euphorbias and the cacti have both evolved almost identical structures to suit the needs of their environments.

Top **Euphorbia griffithii.**

Right **The stems of wood spurge (*Euphorbia amygdaloides*) contain a poisonous white, milky sap.**

Below. **The tiny purple spurge (*Euphorbia peplis*) grows on shingle beaches. The cyathia, containing spherical-shaped glands, are produced in the axils of the leaves.**

Wetlands

Wetlands is a collective term describing habitats that for some or all of the year have their soils waterlogged because the water table is at or very near to the surface of the soil. The three main types of wetland are marshes, bogs and fens. The latter two categories develop over a substratum of peat. If the water supply to the peatlands is rich in nutrients then the area is described as a fen, but where the water supply contains few nutrients it is called a bog.

In tropical areas peat does not form so readily because the higher temperatures result in the plant remains decaying rather than accumulating to form peat layers.

Bogs are often dominated by the many kinds of bog mosses (*Sphagnum* spp.) which thrive in the wet conditions. Of the flowering plants found here, the sedges are the most common, especially in the wetter parts. In slightly drier areas, heathers and whortle-berries (*Vaccinium* spp.) may predominate. Trees are unable to grow because their roots cannot survive in such waterlogged conditions.

Fens are often dominated by reeds such as the common reed (*Phragmites communis*) and reed-maces (*Typha* spp.) which are deeply rooted so they can withstand the flow of water past their stems. The reed is sometimes used for thatching because, although more expensive to use than wheat straw, it has

Below **Within the leaves of sphagnum moss are many empty spaces which can hold large amounts of water.**

Right **Some of the many grasses, sedges and rushes to be found in wetland areas.**

Left **The common reed grows in dense clusters along fenland channels.**

proved to be far more durable and long-lasting.

If the water is still or slow-moving, more weakly rooted species can grow such as bogbean (*Menyanthes trifoliata*) and marsh marigold (*Caltha palustris*). The water level of a fen will often vary and if it drops appreciably shrubs and small trees may be able to colonize. Typical woody species to gain a foothold in these areas are alder (*Alnus* spp.) and buckthorn (*Frangula alnus*). This type of damp woodland is called a carr.

Many areas of fenland have been cleared and drained to provide agricultural land which is very fertile and used for grazing or growing crops. The natural fenland vegetation is then confined to drainage ditches or disappears altogether.

Marshes differ from the previous two categories of wetland mentioned in that they occur over predominantly silt substrates rather than peat. Typical situations for them to occur are river banks, lake shores and deltas. However, their vegetation in many respects is similar to that found in fenlands, and many plant species are common to both.

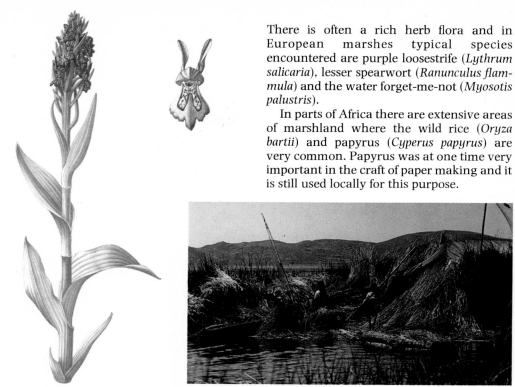

There is often a rich herb flora and in European marshes typical species encountered are purple loosestrife (*Lythrum salicaria*), lesser spearwort (*Ranunculus flammula*) and the water forget-me-not (*Myosotis palustris*).

In parts of Africa there are extensive areas of marshland where the wild rice (*Oryza bartii*) and papyrus (*Cyperus papyrus*) are very common. Papyrus was at one time very important in the craft of paper making and it is still used locally for this purpose.

Above, left **Marsh orchid.**

Above **In some countries reeds are used to make intricately woven boats and even floating houses.**

Left **Papyrus grows high alongside a river in Botswana.**

Opposite **Greater reedmace (*Typha latifolia*). The long, brown female flower-head contains thousands of tiny individual flowers.**

Right **Bogbean can colonise large areas of wetland if the conditions are suitable. The petals are fringed with long, white hairs.**

61

Water Lilies

Many water plants have small, insignificant flowers, but not so the water lilies whose giant blooms grace many a garden pond. They belong to the family Nymphaeaceae and are found throughout the world in lakes, ponds and streams. They belong to a very ancient group of plants and abundant fossil remains have indicated that many of the tropical species grew in Europe before the Ice Age.

The largest water lily of all is the spectacular Queen Victoria water lily (*Victoria amazonica*) from South America whose giant leaves with upturned rims may reach 2m in diameter. The undersurface is strengthened by girder-like ribs and a single leaf can support a weight of 90kg.

Euryale ferox which comes from China and South-east Asia has leaves nearly as big as Victoria, but they lack the upturned rims and are coloured dark violet beneath.

The flowers of water lilies are always solitary and they are usually pollinated by beetles. Many of the tropical species are night-flowering, the blooms only opening at dusk and closing again the next day.

Water lilies have a long history of cultivation. They have been grown for their beauty and also for food, the starchy rhizomes and the roasted seeds being ground into a kind of flour and eaten. Since ancient times many water lilies have had religious associations. It was thought that the large, shining flowers arising from the dark muddy waters represented purity and resurrection. They were extensively cultivated for decorating temples and were revered as sacred objects.

The lovely Indian lotus (*Nelumbo nucifera*) in particular has had a long association with Buddhism, with the belief that Buddha was born in the heart of a lotus flower. The flowers have rose-pink petals which gradually change to a yellowish colour as the flower ages.

The fruit of the water lily contains mucilage which swells when the seeds are ripe to release them. The seeds are large and often have a spongy appendage which traps air bubbles and enables them to float in the water for some time before sinking.

Water lily flowers actually come in a variety of colours many are shades of pink, yellow or white. The lovely *Nymphaea capensis* which is a native of South Africa has petals of a clear blue. Today many beautiful cultivars have been produced by hybridizing different species.

Top Unlike many water lilies, the flower of the lotus is raised well above the water surface on a long, thick stalk.

Middle Lotus flowers are piled high as an offering in a Sri Lankan temple.

Right Queen Victoria water lily.

Above (top) white water lily (***Nymphaea alba***)
(bottom) yellow water lily (***Nuphar lutea***)

Above, left **Water lilies are among the most popular water plants grown in ornamental ponds and lakes.**

Left ***Nymphaea capensis*** **from South Africa.**

Aquatics

There are few types of water that have not successfully been colonized by some species of flowering plants. Whether it be fresh, brackish or salt, still or flowing – they all have an aquatic flora that is specially adapted to a life in water.

Many are rooted at the bottom and remain completely submerged, whilst others emerge above the water surface. A few float in the water unattached, either on the surface or below. The duckweeds are found on the surface of ponds and lakes and are the smallest of all flowering plants with the plant body of one of them, *Wolffia arrhiza*, measuring less than 1mm across. Duckweeds seldom flower but they often successfully colonize new areas by being transported on the feet of water-birds.

Unlike terrestrial plants, aquatics are usually capable of absorbing water through their whole body surface, not just via the

roots. They also have to obtain their oxygen this way, utilizing the oxygen that is dissolved in the water as well as that which they accumulate during the day as a by-product of photosynthesis. The oxygen present in water is at much lower concentrations than are available to their terrestrial relatives and many water plants have special spongy tissues called aerenchyma to help the oxygen diffuse more easily throughout the plant.

It is quite common for water plants to have two shapes of leaves, those that are submerged being different from those that float on, or are raised above, the water surface. The submerged leaves are either very long and narrow or they are finely dissected into narrow strands. Both these forms offer less resistance to flowing water than a broader leaf and prevent the foliage being torn to shreds by the force of the water. The floating leaves are usually oval or broadly rounded in outline with a thick waxy covering on their upper surface to repel water.

Most water plants, even the submerged ones, raise their flowers above the surface of the water, where they can be pollinated by the wind or by insects. This occurs because most pollen is harmed by immersion in water and only a very few water plants such as the hornwort (*Ceratophyllum demersum*) have water-resistant pollen which can float along in the water to fertilize the female flowers.

Under suitable conditions many aquatics will produce a luxurience of growth that is quite unrivalled among land plants, and this can sometimes cause problems. The water hyacinth (*Eichhornia crassipes*) is a very attractive water plant which originally came

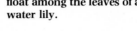

Above **Duckweed plants float among the leaves of a water lily.**

Left **Water hyacinth (*Eichhornia crassipes*).**

Right **Arrowhead has three types of leaves. Those produced underwater are long and straplike. Others float on the water surface and are broader in outline. The aerial leaves are different altogether, shaped like large arrowheads.**

Above **Attempts are now being made to find a solution to the rapid spread of water hyacinth.**

from tropical America. It was introduced into many waterways, often with disastrous results because it spread so rapidly that the water became choked with the result that irrigation canals, drainage ditches and rice fields became useless. It reproduces vegetatively at an incredible rate, being capable of doubling its numbers within a fortnight.

Below **Frogbit (*Hydrocharis morsus-ranae*) grows in the still water of ponds and ditches.**

Seashore/Coastal Plants

Seashores may be sandy, rocky, marshy or shingly, but whatever the type, plants that live in coastal habitats must be tolerant of a high concentration of salt, both in the soil and in the surrounding air. Those plants that can do this are called halophytes.

The eel-grasses *Zostera* and *Posidonia* are among a tiny group of flowering plants that are able to live below the level of the low-tide mark in a permanently saline aquatic habitat.

The majority of halophytes live further up the shore or on cliffs where they are rarely subjected to complete immersion in salt water, though they still have many problems to face.

The soils often contain little in the way of nutrients and have a high percentage of salt which makes water uptake by the roots more difficult due to the higher osmotic pressure. They are subjected to strong inshore winds carrying salt and sand which blasts the leaves. As a protection many have either a hard surface or a covering of wax to prevent the salt being absorbed. The sea holly (*Eryngium maritimum*), a member of the Umbelliferae family and one of the most attractive coastal plants has bluish-tinged leaves which are hard and spiny. It grows about 30 to 60cm and has globular heads of pale blue flowers.

Others, such as the sea sage (*Tournefortia gnaphalodes*), protect themselves by having a thick layer of hairs covering their leaves, which prevents the salt from coming into contact with their surface. The salt is deposited instead as crystals on the tips of the hairs, to fall away harmlessly when the hairs dry out.

Salt-resistant plants play an important role along the coast where there are sand dunes. Their roots help to bind the dune together and prevent the sand being blown inshore and swamping large areas of lowland. Perhaps the most important plant in this respect is the marram grass (*Ammophila arenaria*) whose extensive root system grows down through the sand in search of water from below. It has been extensively planted in Britain and other countries and appears to thrive even though it is often covered by sand.

The leaves of marram grass have the ability to roll-up due to the presence of special hinge cells on the inner surface of the leaf. When the marram grass has sufficient water to meet its requirements the hinge cells swell causing the leaf to unroll. Any drop in the plant's moisture level results in the guard cells collapsing and the leaf rolling up. When the leaf is in a rolled-up position all the stomata, the tiny pores through which water is lost, are located on the inner surface of the leaf between a series of folds. As a further protection against excessive evaporation there are numerous stiff hairs positioned on the outer surfaces of the folds. The outer surface of the leaf has no stomata and is protected by a thick cuticle.

After many years the dune vegetation slowly changes. As plants die their remains gradually increase the organic content of the sand and this will provide suitable conditions of growth for new plants to become established. The extra organic content of the sand will also increase its water retention capabilities and various small herbs will gain a foothold. Eventually some shrubs such as sea buckthorn (*Hippohaë rhamnoides*) and privet (*Ligustrum vulgare*) may grow on these dunes.

In tropical areas *Ipomoea pes-caprae*, a member of the bindweed family (Convolvulaceae) is an important coloniser of sandy seashores, together with the grass *Spinifex littoreus*, which grows in tufts along the shore.

Below **Flowerheads of sea holly contain many tiny flowers.**

Below, right **The horned-poppy is an attractive seashore plant which thrives on shingle banks.**

Right, above **Stiff foliage of the marram grass is a familiar sight along many stretches of coast.**

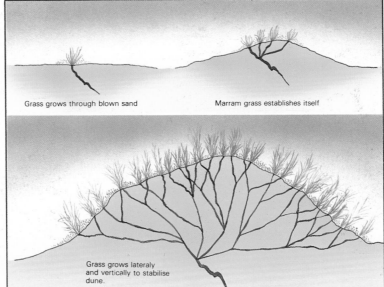

Grass grows through blown sand

Marram grass establishes itself

Grass grows lateraly and vertically to stabilise dune.

Above **Sea Buckthorn.**

Left As sand accumulates around the base of the marram grass, the underground stems continue to grow upwards and outwards to prevent the whole plant being buried.

Right The sprawling stems of sea bindweed (*Calystegia soldanella*) trail over the upper parts of the seashore.

67

Parasites

Most plants are self-sufficient in terms of food production, since they use the process of photosynthesis to manufacture sugars and other foods from carbon dioxide and water. But a few plants have forsaken self-sufficiency for the less demanding, but more risky, life of parasitism. Parasites rely on their hosts for some or all of their nutritional requirements and the balance between parasite and host is a delicate one. If the parasite takes more than the host can easily provide, both may die.

There are successive levels of parasitism, from plants which will take advantage of a chance to augment their own efforts, to complete or obligate parasites, which are totally dependent on their hosts. This suc-

cession is accompanied by a reduction in the body of the parasite so that some are barely recognisable as plants unless they are in flower.

Hemiparasites look little different to normal plants and are only partly dependant on a host. They have functional green leaves and manufacture at least some of their own foods; only the roots are modified to rob the host of water and minerals. Many members of the Scrophulariaceae such as eyebrights (*Euphrasia* species) and witch weeds (*Striga* species) are hemiparasites, attaching their roots to those of the host plants, principally grasses and cereals. The best known hemiparasites are the mistletoes. They attach

themselves to trees, commonly on a branch, by means of suckers formed from the modified roots. The suckers, called haustoria, penetrate the conducting system of the branch and draw off water and minerals to meet the mistletoe's needs.

Obligate parasites take food as well as water and minerals from the host plant. Their leaves are very reduced, even absent and, having no need for chlorophyll, are usually reddish or brown rather than green. Unlike hemiparasites which have quite catholic tastes, obligate parasites are frequently host specific, able to live only on members of a single species.

Broomrapes (*Orobanche* species) and mem-

bers of the Balanophoraceae (which have no English names) attach their haustoria to the roots of their hosts. Unlike those of hemiparasites, the leaves are reduced to scales and the plants completely lack green pigmentation. The only part of the plants to emerge above ground are the flower spikes. Those of broomrapes bear flowers with subdued colours and a few brown, scale-like leaves. Despite their name, broomrapes parasitise other plants besides broom, for example ivy. The Balanophoraceae have brightly coloured inflorescences of greatly reduced flowers. These develop within underground tubers, sometimes not bursting out until the flowers are already open. When the inflores-

Below The flower heads of *Balanophoraceae* are often fleshy looking and fungus-like.

The mistletoe

This rather woody, yellow-green evergreen is perhaps the best known of our semi-parasitic plants. It occurs most commonly on trees in the south east and the west Midlands, where it mainly grows high up on the branches of oak and poplar. It also occurs frequently in old orchards on apple trees. More rarely it will grow on beech, birch and plane, but on these trees the smoothness of the bark is probably unsuitable for its establishment. The plant is only semi-parasitic as its leaves contain chlorophyll and it can therefore carry out photosynthesis and produce its own carbohydrates. It is dependent on the host tree for water and inorganic nutrients and well as some extra carbohydrate. These substances are absorbed by means of suckers which are forced into the tissues of the host. Although the flowers are inconspicuous and rarely noticed, fleshy white berries are frequently produced. These berries are attractive to birds, particularly thrushes, hence the name mistle thrush. The seeds may stick to their beaks, and so be carried to another tree. They are then implanted when the bird cleans its beak by rubbing it on the new branch.

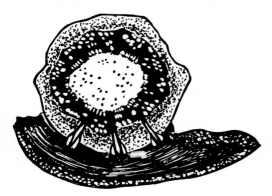

Above A section through the stems of a dodder and its host. The haustoria of the dodder can be seen as conical shapes within the host stem.

Opposite, top One of the strangest plant paras es is *Rafflesia*.

Opposite Greater broomrape (*Orobanche repurrgenstore*) attacks shrubby legumes. H e its brownish flower spikes can be seen amor st the bright yellow flowers of the host.

cences reach the surface they have a very curious appearance, resembling fungi more than flowers!

Dodders (*Cuscuta* species) are unusual in being stem parasites. They are little more than reddish, thread-like stems with a few scale leaves and small heads of tightly packed flowers. When a newly germinated seedling encounters a potential host its stem rapidly twines up that of the host. If the host is suitable the dodder inserts haustoria into the host tissue. The root of the dodder then atrophies and the parasite grows without any further contact with the soil.

Perhaps the most insidious parasite is *Rafflesia* which comes from South-east Asia. The body of this plant is represented only by a web-like system of tissue which spreads throughout the growth-cells of the host — usually a tropical vine. The only parts recognisable as a flowering plant are the flowers themselves. These are the largest in the world and can measure up to one metre across. They are the colour of rotting flesh and produce an odour to match — a combination which attracts pollinating insects.

The figwort family (*Scrophulariaceae*) contain many hemiparasitic species. In general they are similar to normal plants but their roots batten on to those of other species. Eyebrights (*below*) and yellow rattle (*right*) are both found in areas such as downland where they parasitise grasses.

Plant Distribution

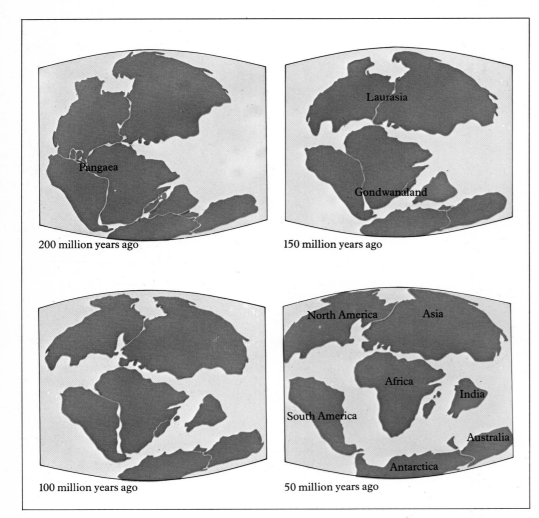

200 million years ago

150 million years ago

100 million years ago

50 million years ago

Plants are not evenly distributed throughout the world. Some occupy large areas of the globe; others are restricted to a few small areas or to only one area. Why should this be so?

Part of the answer lies with the different methods of dispersal. Some plants are capable of long-range dispersal, across even oceans. Others are very limited in their capabilities and cannot spread quickly or far.

Another part of the answer is provided by climatic conditions. Plants only grow where the habitats for which they are adapted occur.

Man has radically altered the natural distribution of many species, mainly by his effects on the environment. However, man is a recent factor; more distant events which are explained by the history of the world have also had a great influence on the distribution of plants today.

Continental drift

The earth's crust, including continents and ocean basins, is composed of a number of plates. These plates are in slow but continuous motion — a phenomenon called continental drift.

Before arriving at their present positions the continents were joined in a single landmass, Pangaea. Their subsequent separation allowed independent evolution and divergence of their plant groups. Laurasia and Gondwanaland separated first but each remained intact for a while so that North America and Europe have more groups in common with each other than with southern continents and vice versa. Separation continued and movement of some continents to new latitudes affected many groups. Penninsula India for example drifted northwards across tropical regions, losing many of the ancestral groups it shared with the southern continents on its journey towards eventual collision with Asia. The situation in Antarctica was more extreme, its drift to the south pole destroying all plant life there.

The last ice-age

During the last ice-age (some two million years ago) major ice-sheets advanced over much of North America, Europe and Northern Asia. In the Southern Hemisphere the Andes, South Island New Zealand and probably South-east Australia, as well as Antarctica, had large glaciers.

The effect on plants was profound, causing world-wide migrations. In North America, for example, the plants retreated before the ice to southern refuges from which they later spread north again. In Europe, however, the Mediterranean and the major mountain ranges run east-west and form natural barriers which cut off the route to safety. Many warmth-loving plants were eliminated and never recolonized these areas.

Left, above Mountain avens (*Dryas octopetala*) is common throughout the arctic but further south it is found only in high mountain ranges.

Left Members of the *Proteaceae* such as this *Dryandra* are found mainly in the Austral realm.

When the ice retreated cold-adapted species moved north again to the Arctic but some were stranded in mountain regions such as the Alps where they survived by moving up into higher, cooler altitudes. This explains the similarity between the arctic and alpine floras of today.

Floristic realms

The world can be divided into four realms based on the different composition of their floras. Some plant families are common to more than one realm, but others are unique to particular realms.

The Holarctic is separated from the Paleo-tropic by the mountain chains of the Atlas, Taurus and Himalayas. The division of the Holarctic by the Bering Strait is very recent (in geological terms) and the two halves, North America and Eurasia, have many plant groups in common.

Some families, such as the palms, mangroves and camelias grow throughout the tropics but there is a definite floristic division between the Old (Palaeotropic) and New World (Neotropic) regions, reflecting the very long separation of these areas.

The smallest — and most fragmented — of the four is the Austral realm. South America and South Africa are very distinct from the remainder of these two continents and their floras have features in common with those of Australia and New Zealand.

Left **Each floral realm is defined by the presence of particular plant families within its boundaries. Conifers such as these Serbian spruces typify the Holarctic realm.**

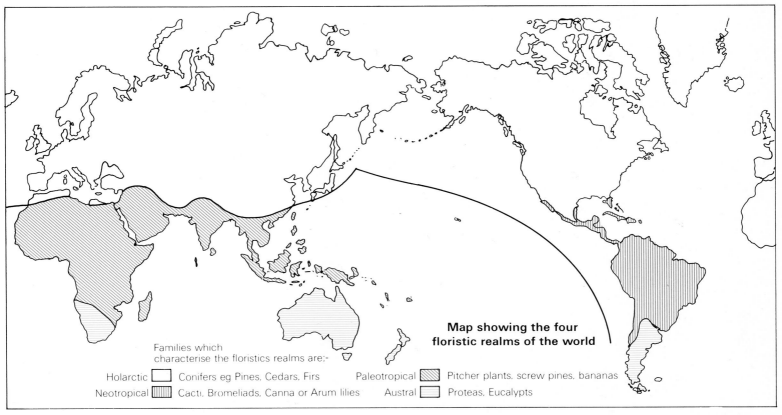

Map showing the four floristic realms of the world

Families which characterise the floristics realms are:-

Holarctic ☐ Conifers eg Pines, Cedars, Firs

Neotropical ▦ Cacti, Bromeliads, Canna or Arum lilies

Paleotropical ▨ Pitcher plants, screw pines, bananas

Austral ▤ Proteas, Eucalypts

Islands

Above **The dragon tree (*Dracaena draco*) has disappeared from many parts of its former range but it survives on islands such as the Canaries, where it is often grown in parks.**

Left **Because of their isolation oceanic islands may develop their own unique floras.**

Following man's interference formerly lush parts of St. Helena are now almost bare.

Some of the world's most fascinating floras are to be found on islands. We usually think of islands as remote pieces of land surrounded by water. But a single mountain surrounded by plains can be an island for alpine plants, and a lake or pond or even a patch of woodland in the centre of a field is equally an island to the plants which inhabit it.

Botanically the most interesting islands are oceanic ones, that is islands separated from the nearest land by great expanses of ocean. Continental islands, such as Britain, have often had recent connections with the nearby landmasses and share a similar, though usually poorer, flora with their neighbouring continents.

Because their extreme isolation causes problems for colonisation, oceanic islands have relatively few species. Those that are present face less competition, evolving in isolation and adapting and diversifying in different ways, often to a far greater extent than their mainland relatives. The ocean barriers that prevent immigration also prevent emmigration and so these new species are confined to the islands and add to their fascination. Species like this, which are found in only one area of the world, are known as endemics and old island floras are

particularly rich in them. In New Zealand around three-quarters of the plants are endemic and in Hawaii an even greater proportion, ninety per cent, are found nowhere else in the world.

Not all islands of course have a rich endemic flora. Iceland for example, has not been free from the grip of ice long enough to develop distinctive species of its own.

Another reason for the importance of, and interest in, islands is their role as refuges for plants. Many islands have a long history of stable climate. While continental areas have undergone great — and for plants often disastrous — changes, islands such as the Canaries and Madagascar have remained unaffected. This has allowed the survival there of plants which have disappeared from other parts of the world. The Canary Islands and Madeira support a number of relict species — plants which were formerly much more widespread, but which have died out in large areas of their original range.

Oceanic islands are generally small with few resources. Because of their isolation, losses are not easily made up if the original flora is destroyed. They are delicately balanced systems prone to rapid destruction if interfered with and many have suffered at the hands of man.

The greatest risk is from the introduction of grazing animals new to the islands and against which the plants are not adapted. When discovered in 1501 the Atlantic island of St Helena was covered in luxuriant ebony forest. The introduction of goats began the destruction, hastened by logging, which by 1810 had left the island almost bare. The St Helena ebony is only one of the island's many endemics which are now extinct.

Above Echiums grow throughout most of mainland Europe and Asia, but the giant *E. wildprettii* is a spectacular species found only on the island of Tenerife. These plants are approximately $1\frac{1}{2}$m high!

Above **For any land mass its potential for colonisation depends on its size, since larger islands are likely to have a more varied range of habitats than smaller ones. Thus the larger the island the more species are found on it. This general rule applies to islands wherever their location in the world.**

Below **Members of the genus *Argyranthemum* are relict species confined to the oceanic islands off West Africa.**

Below **The Canary Islands have many endemic plants, especially members of the daisy family such as *Lugoa revoluta*.**

Conservation

Estimates of the number of different species of flowering plants vary a great deal and is impossible to calculate accurately; however, the figure probably falls somewhere between 220 000 and 300 000. Of these, nobody knows just how many have already become extinct, but it has been estimated that by the end of the next century, one in ten of the flowering plants will be in danger of disappearing altogether.

Plants particularly threatened are those with restricted distributions such as the climbing jade vine (Strongylodon macrobotrys) *from the Philippines with its graceful inflorescences containing as many as a hundred flowers of the strangest blue-green colour.*

The world's flora is not evenly distributed throughout, tropical areas being richer in species than temperate regions. However, until recently it has been in the temperate regions that most research has been centred and so now, with tropical forests being destroyed at the rate of 250 000 hectares per year as they are felled for timber and cleared to provide land for growing crops, species are being lost before they have even been named and fully studied.

Many of the endangered plants are very beautiful and are worth conserving for that aspect alone, considering the amount of pleasure we derive from looking at them. However, there is a far more important and fundamental reason for conserving our plant life – we could not exist without it and who knows what hidden uses remain to be discovered – perhaps new medicinal drugs, new foods or substitutes for existing chemicals that are in short supply. Once a species becomes extinct its unique characters are lost forever, and that is a tragedy.

Hedgehog cactus (*Echinocereus engelmanii*) and brittle bush (*Encelis farinosa*) at Oregon Pipe Cactus National Monument, Montana, U.S.A.

Overleaf Meadow flowers in southern England.

Places to Visit

Below is a list of some of the world's leading arboreta and botanic gardens.

Australia
Adelaide Botanic Garden, South Australia
Brisbane Botanic Garden, Queensland
Canberra Botanic Garden
Melbourne Botanic Gardens, South Yarra, Victoria
Sydney Botanic Garden, New South Wales
Royal Tasmanian Botanic Gardens, Hobart, Tasmania

Britain
National Pinetum, Bedgebory, Kent
The Botanic Gardens, Bath
University Botanic Garden, Cambridge
Dawyck Arboretum, Stobo, Peebles, Scotland
Royal Botanic Gardens, Kew, Richmond, Surrey
Royal Horticultural Society's Garden, Wisley, Guildford
Wakehurst Place, Sussex
The University of Liverpool Botanic Garden, Ness, Wirral
Westonbirt Arboretum, near Tetbury, Gloucestershire
Borde Hill Gardens, Haywards Heath
The Hillier Arboretum, Romsey, Hants.

Canada
Dominion Arboretum, Ottawa
Montreal Botanical Garden, Montreal
Royal Botanic Garden, Hamilton, Ontario

Ireland
Castlewelland Forest Park, County Down, Northern Ireland
National Botanic Gardens, Glasnevin, Dublin

New Zealand
Albert Park, Auckland
Botanic Gardens, Christchurch
Botanic Gardens, Dunedin
Kaingaroa State Forest, Rotorua
Pukeiti Rhododendron Trust, New Plymouth
Waipoua Kauri Forest, Northland
Botanical Gardens, Wellington

United Sates of America
Arnold Arboretum, Harvard University, Jamaica Plain, Massachusetts
Highland and Durand-Eastman Parks, Rochester, New York
Missouri Botanical Garden, Gray Summit, St. Louis, Missouri
Morton Arboretum, Lisle, Illinois
National Arboretum, Washington, DC
University of Washington Arboretum, Seattle, Washington
University of California Botanic Garden, Berkeley, California
Brooklyn Botanic Garden and Arboretum, Brooklyn, New York
Longwood Gardens, Kennett Square, Pennsylvania
The Holden Arboretum, Mentor, Ohio
The New York Botanic Garden, Bronx, New York
Morris Arboretum, Philadelphia, Pennsylvania

Belgium
Jardin Botanique National de Belgique, Brussels
Arboretum, Kalmthout

Denmark
Arboretet, Hørsholm, Denmark

Finland
Arboretum Mustila, Elimaki, Finland

France
Jardin Botanic de la Ville, Lyon, Rhône
Jardin des plantes de l'Université de Montpellier, Montpellier
Arborètum des Barres et Fructicetum Vilmorinianum, Nugent-sur-Vernisson, Loiret

Japan
Aritaki Arboretum, Ko-shigaya-shi, Saitama-ken

Holland
Wageningen

Sweden
Goteborgs Botaniska Tradgard, Goteborg
The Botanical Garden, Uppsala

Further Reading

Barneby, T. P., **European Alpine Flowers in Colour**, Thomas Nelson & Sons Ltd. 1967

Barthlott, W. **Cacti**. Stanley Thornes (Publishers) Ltd. 1979

Bellamy, David, **Botanic Man**. Hamlyn 1980

Duddington, C. L., **Evolution in Plant Design**, Faber and Faber Ltd. 1969

Emsley, Michael, **Rain Forests and Cloud Forests**, Harry N. Abrams Inc. New York 1979

Everard, Barbara and Morley, Brian D., **Wild Flowers of the World**, Peerage Books 1970

Gleason, H. A. and Cronquist, Arthur, **The Natural Geography of Plants**, Columbia University Press, New York 1964

Graaf, HanJan de and Hyams, Edward, **Lilies**, Thomas Nelson & Sons Ltd. 1967

Heywood, V. H. (ed.), **Flowering Plants of the World**, Oxford University Press 1978

Heywood, V. H. and Chant, S. R., **Popular Encyclopedia of Plants**, Cambridge University Press 1982

Huxley, Anthony, **Plant and Planet**, Penguin 1978

Kuijt, J. **The Biology of Parasitic Flowering Plants**, University of California Press 1969

Moore, David (ed.), **Green Planet**, Cambridge University Press 1982

Moore, Ian, **Grass and Grasslands**, Collins 1966

Pijl, L. van der and Dodson, Calaway H., **Orchid Flowers**, University of Miami Press 1966

Proctor, John and Susan, **Nature's Use of Colour in Plants and their Flowers**, Peter Lowe 1978

Proctor, Michael and Yeo, Peter, **The Pollination of Flowers**, Collins 1973

Richards, P. W., **The Tropical Rain Forest**, Cambridge University Press 1981

Rauh, Werner, **Bromeliads**, Blandford Press 1979

Sculthorpe, C. D., **The Biology of Aquatic Vascular Plants**, Edward Arnold (Publishers) Ltd. 1967

Slack, Adrian, **Carnivorous Plants**, Ebury Press 1979

Swindells, Philip, **Waterlilies**, Timber Press 1983

Thomas, Barry, **The Evolution of Plants and Flowers**, Peter Lowe 1981

Tribe, Ian, **The Plant Kingdom**, Hamlyn 1970

Vankat, John, **The Natural Vegetation of North America**, John Wiley & Sons 1979

Index